I0832657

VIEW OF STAR ISLAND.

THE

ISLES OF SHOALS.

AN

HISTORICAL SKETCH.

BY

JOHN SCRIBNER JENNESS.

NEW YORK:
PUBLISHED BY HURD AND HOUGHTON.
Cambridge: The Riverside Press.
1873.

RIVERSIDE, CAMBRIDGE:
STEREOTYPED AND PRINTED BY
H. O. HOUGHTON AND COMPANY.

INTRODUCTION.

THE cluster of rocks, known as the *Isles of Shoals*, which rise out of the ocean some two leagues from the mainland of New Hampshire, enjoy a preference, as a summer resort, over all the other islets which stud the Gulf of Maine. Hither come yearly, and in increasing throngs, great multitudes of people from all parts of the country, to refresh their jaded spirits in the cool solitude, the healing silence, of these barren rocks.

The islands are not, in themselves, more attractive, perhaps, than many others on the New England coast. They are but stacks of bulging granite, weather-bleached, tossed over with boulders of all sizes, ragged and torn on the edges where they confront the ocean, and everywhere of a broken, irregular surface. No smooth ground is upon them, except a few acres of mowing land on Haley's, and a few small vegetable gardens upon Star. They are wholly destitute of trees, and even of shrubs, except huckleberry and bayberry bushes, woodbines, wildroses, and such like, wherever in the crevices of the rocks the shallow roots have found a handful of soil. Moreover, this dearth of vegetable life is naturally accompanied by a scarcity of animal life. Land animals are rarely seen; singing birds find little here to attract their stay. The stillness of the Islands, in calm weather, is profound; their barrenness absolute.

The reason of the preference these bare Islets have acquired as a "*watering place*," is not, however, far to seek. It is to be found chiefly in their climate.

The easterly winds that sweep landward over New England, are caught in the north by the long coast of Acadia and Maine, and emptied into Casco Bay; while, on the south, the projecting arms of Cape Cod and Cape Ann gather them up and pour them into the "Bay of the Massachusetts." Thence come the cheerless fogs, and mists, and soaking rains, which visit so frequently the region of Boston and Portland, while, at the same time, the shores of New Hampshire, at an equal distance between these cities, rejoice in clear skies and gentle breezes. Impressed with the importance of this circumstance, we have taken pains to collate such meteorological observations at those three points as were accessible. The results show a wider discrepancy than we had suspected.

According to the careful observations taken by the officers of the Medical department of the army, at Fort Preble in Portland Harbor, Fort Constitution at Newcastle, and Fort Independence at Boston, during the period from 1831 to 1843, it turns out, that while there are during the year, on the average, fifty-eight rainy days at Portland, and nearly fifty-eight at Boston, there are but twenty-five at the Piscataqua. The mean annual rain-fall at Portland is thirty-seven inches, at Boston forty-two inches, and at Portsmouth but thirty inches. On the other hand, while the average temperature of the summer months is at Portland 66° Fahr., and at Boston 68°, that of Portsmouth is but 63°. The mean annual range of temperature at Fort Preble is 100.66° Fahr., at Fort Independence in Boston 96.75°, at Portsmouth 92.20°; the bleak easterly winds blow on the average at Portland 86 days in the year, at Boston 118 days, at Portsmouth but 81 days.[1]

It is this marked superiority of New Hampshire over her neighbors in respect of climate, that has brought the coast of that state into great and growing favor

[1] Meteorolog. Reg. for U. S., pp. 322, 324.

as a summer resort; and as the knowledge of that superiority of climate shall extend, the multitude of summer visitors to her mainland and adjacent islands, will, we predict, continue to increase indefinitely.

The Isles of Shoals thus depend very largely upon the exceptional beauty of their summer climate for their charm. Seated within dim view of the mainland, the summer winds from all quarters are tempered and refreshed by the wide expanse of ocean around them; the thermometer is singularly steady; sudden changes are rare;[1] the skies are clear; the sea is blue and bright; pleasant breezes cool the blood and brace the nerves, and sleep is relaxed and soothed by the perpetual plash of a slumberous ocean. Sometimes, indeed, the tempest rises in its wrath and awakes old ocean from its repose, and then, for a space, the uproar of the elements is appalling; but this fierce mood is not the habitual temper of the place during the summer months. Those who love to witness Nature in her wild and angry humor, should visit her here in the December storms.

None of the group are of any considerable size. The total area of the cluster, seven or eight in number,

[1] So strangely equable is the temperature, especially during the summer, that visitors are said sometimes to suspect the mercury has been craftily removed from the thermometers, and the tube painted to stand always at 65°.

does not exceed, says Williamson, 600 acres; of which, Appledore, formerly Hog Island, is the largest, being about a mile in length from east to west, and five-eighths of a mile across. Smutty Nose, or Haley's Island, is next in size, about a mile long and half a mile in width. These two islands, together with Malaga, Cedar, and Duck Islands, belong to the State of Maine. The next in size to Smutty Nose, is Star Island, on which formerly stood the town of Gosport,—on the New Hampshire side of the line. "It is three-fourths of a mile long from N. W. to S. E., and half a mile wide."

The harbor of the Shoals — enclosed between Appledore, Haley's, Cedar, and Star Islands,— furnishes a tolerably secure refuge for small vessels "in distress of weather." With a view of improving this little port, Mr. Samuel Haley constructed about the beginning of the present century, a sea-wall between Smutty Nose (now named after him *Haley's Island*), and the small rock on its north, called Malaga. In 1821, the United States Government reconstructed and improved this wall, and also built another of considerable length from Smutty Nose to Cedar Island on the south. While this latter sea-wall stood, it furnished a great protection to the enclosed anchorage ground; but the contractor, Mr.

Thomas Haven, of Portsmouth, was unable, with the scanty appropriation at his command, ($2,500), to build it sufficiently solid to resist the tremendous attacks of the ocean under a north-east storm. A few years after the sea-wall had been completed, it was overthrown so thoroughly, that hardly a vestige of it is now remaining; only a part of its course being discernable at low water. Lying, however, as the harbor does, under the lee of Appledore, Smutty Nose and Malaga, it affords a tolerable shelter for the fishing craft and coasters who still take refuge there. It is to be hoped that the U. S. Government, in view of the great importance of this little harbor as a refuge from our frequent easterly storms, will, ere long, make an appropriation adequate to the permanent restoration of the Cedar Island sea-wall. A comparatively trifling sum would be needed for this purpose.

It is not our purpose, in these pages, to enter upon any detailed description of these noted Islets. The magazines and newspapers have of late years abounded with articles on that subject. Poetry and romance have chosen these rocks as favorite themes. Whittier, Hawthorne, and Lowell have illumined them with the magical light of their genius; and above all, the pencil of Mrs. Celia Thaxter has portrayed their sublimity and picturesque beauty with so much both of vigor and delicacy, that nothing is left to be desired.

The general interest of the public in these Islets might, however, be pleased, we have thought, with a fuller account of their *early* history than has hitherto been furnished. The Shoals have never enjoyed their local antiquary. A few facts and anecdotes concerning them were gathered up, in 1800, by the Rev. Jedidiah Morse, and published in the Mass. Hist. Collections; Williamson, in his history of Maine, has reproduced this essay with slight additions; the Coast Survey Reports may have contributed a little more, and in the collections of our various Antiquarian Societies, allusions to the group may be found, sparsely scattered here and there; but the reader will in vain seek, amid these jejune and trivial materials, for much of instruction or entertainment. It is only from the ancient town and Provincial Records, the statutes, documents and correspondence which have descended to us, as well as from the careful study of general American and European chronicles, that any thorough local history of the Isles of Shoals can, at the present day, be compiled.

Such a task would, however, be laborious to the writer, while the minute relation of petty occurences among a community of fishermen and sailors, especially now that the entire population has been swept away, must needs prove wearisome to the general reader.

It is our utmost hope, that some selections from the highly romantic early annals of the Isles of Shoals, together with a brief sketch of the social, moral, and religious condition of the motley, shifting population, who formerly in large numbers inhabited these rocks, may serve to while away a vacant hour or two of some summer idler, amid these once busy scenes.

CHAMPLAIN.

ISLES OF SHOALS.

CHAPTER I.

THE Isles of Shoals played a more important part in the early history of New England, than the general reader would probably imagine. Long before the landing of the Pilgrim Fathers, these barren rocks were visited and described by the French and English navigators, and were the annual resort of fishermen from Virginia and maritime Europe. Indeed, when we consider that during the entire sixteenth century, fleets of fishing vessels yearly visited our eastern waters, we are justified in conjecturing, that for many lustres of years anterior to the settlement of New England, the commodiousness of the Isles of Shoals for the prosecution of the fisheries must have, summer after summer, attracted thither the Doggers and Pinckes of the English; the clumsey Busses of Holland and Zealand, the light Fly-Boats of Flanders, the Biskiner, and the Portingal, and many another of those odd high-peaked vessels, whose models seem so quaint, and whose rig is so incomprehensible to us of the present day.

The first unmistakable mention of these Islets falls, however, within the succeeding century. There can be little doubt they were sighted by Gosnold in 1602, and by Martin Pring in 1603; but it is not until the voyage of the French along our coast in 1605, that a distinct reference to them is made in the chronicles.

In 1603, the French monarch, Henry of Navarre, being desirous of extending his dominions in the New World, granted to Pierre de Guast, sieur de Monts, a patent for the entire territory from the 40th to the 46th degree of North Latitude — embracing thus the whole of our present New England.[1] The next year (1604), de Monts, accompanied by Samuel Champlain de Brouage, and a considerable party of emigrants, sailed from France, to take possession of the granted territory; and coasting along the rock-bound shores of Nova Scotia and New Brunswick, landed at last on the Island of St. Croix (now called *Neutral Island*), in Passamaquoddy Bay. Here de Monts set up

[1] Murdock, Hist. of Nova Scotia, Vol. I., p. 22.

the royal standard of France, and passed the winter. The next summer, (1605), he resolved to seek a warmer climate for the permanent foundation of his French colony.

Accordingly, he undertook a voyage of discovery to the southward, in a pinnace of fifteen tons, which he had built at St. Croix Island, during the winter,—the firstling, probably, of our American marine. In his company went Champlain, the chronicler of the voyage, Champdoré, the master, and a crew of about twenty sailors and soldiers.

As the waters to be traversed were little known to them, the pinnace was piloted along the coast by a young Indian of Acadia, named *Panounias*,[1] and his lately wedded squaw, "whom," says Champlain, "he did not wish to part from."[2] Panounias was of the Souriquois, or Micmac, tribe who inhabited Acadia, but his gentle spouse came from the hostile Armouchiquois of the western coast. Her mother's wigwam had been pitched near the Chouahouet, or Saco River. It was in the course of his stolen visits by sea to the Indian maiden, that Panounias had, doubtless, become familiar with the coast from the Oigudi (or St. John's) to the Saco River. From headland to headland,

[1] *Panoniac*, according to L'Escarbot.

[2] Les Voyages de Champlain, Quebec ed., Vol. III., p. 45.

Panounias now pointed out the course to de Monts and Champlain; through the thousand islets along the coast, he threaded the way; he led them into the harbors, and piloted them up the rivers, and showed them where provisions and sweet waters were to be had. The cruise was most prosperous and delightful; the Indian girl, who stood by the side of Panounias in the prow of the pinnace, proved, indeed, a very Halcyon of the seas. Soft breezes wafted the bark everywhere over a smiling ocean, and the light of moon and stars gleamed tranquilly by night on its surface.

Sometimes, bands of the natives would come down to the shore, and, with every token of amity, would dance and gambol beside the vessel, for miles along the sands; sometimes, Panounias and his bride would be set ashore to hold *tabagie*, or council, with them, and to carry them presents; and then, says the chronicler, "*ils redaunserent mieux qu' auparavant*," (they danced better than ever).

And now comes the yachting party to Richman's Island, near Casco Bay; and there they find such abundance of grapes, that they name it "L'isle de Bacchus"; the natives gather around them, and the night is spent in mirth and revelry.

Next day the pinnace swept along to Chouahouet,

now Saco; and there they met with bands of musicians, who could play rustic melodies upon flageolets made out of reeds or cornstalks, "*en gambadant*," says L'Esçarbot, "*selon leur coutume*,"[1] (gambolling, as they are wont).

Shortly after, they landed at Cape Porpoise, named by Champlain, "Le Port aux isles," and here they were charmed with the glad song of infinite numbers of blackbirds and bob-o-links; and thence to the Kennebunk River, where they were astonished with the immense flocks of turtle doves or wild pigeons.

On the 15th day of July, 1605, the French navigators sailed smoothly on from Cape Porpoise twelve leagues toward the south; they coasted along the beaches of Maine and New Hampshire, passing the Piscataqua River without notice, and by nightfall, had reached Great Boar's Head in Hampton. Finding no harbor there, they again put to sea, a couple of leagues, and looked about them in the twilight. What they saw shall be better given in the language of Champlain, for his words are the first written description, however brief, of the Isles of Shoals.

"*Nous apperceusmes un cap a la grande terre au su quart du suest de nous, ou il pourioit avoir quelque six lieues; a l'est deux lieues, apperceusmes trois*

[1] Hist. de la Nouv. France, Vol. II., p. 562.

ou quatre isles asses hautes, et a l'ouest, un grand cu de sac."

"We saw a cape, bearing south, a quarter southwest from us, distant some eighteen miles; on the east, two leagues distant, we saw three or four rather prominent islands, and on the west Ipswitch Bay." The three or four "*isles asses hautes,*" spoken of by Champlain, were our present Isles of Shoals.

After, this, the French navigators sailed on as far as Long Island Sound, and thence returned to Acadia, without having selected any particular spot in New England for a settlement. The following year they renewed their search, but with the same lack of success, and from that time, the French turned their eyes wholly to the St. Lawrence and Canada; Champlain, in 1608, founded Quebec, and New England was left unoccupied, to be some years later colonized by the English.

Had de Monts and Champlain been moved by the virgin charms of New England, it is quite certain the flood of French emigration would have been diverted to her shores, and she would have embraced for ages, perhaps even to the present time, the fortunes of the French people; the French language would have been heard to-day on the banks of the Piscataqua, and over the rocks of Champlain's "*isles asses hautes*," the vivacity of French manners would have startled the precise streets of Boston itself, and the Jesuit or the Franciscan would have celebrated high mass upon her altars.

Some of our readers may perhaps regard this rescue of New England, as a *Remarkable Providence*,— particularly those who are not much acquainted with France.

The melancholy fate of poor Panounias, who piloted the French pinnace so happily past the "*isles asses hautes*," must not be passed over unlamented. Only two years afterwards, his bride was called to bewail his cold-blooded murder at the hands of her own jealous kindred. Panounias had gone, in his canoe, to the Saco River, upon a trading voyage with some goods of de Monts. He was there treacherously set upon by the warriors of the Armouchiquois, and put to death; in retaliation, they pretended, for injuries inflicted on them by some of Panounias' tribe in Acadia.

The corpse of the murdered brave was, however, rescued from their fury, and carried back by the faithful Ouagimou to Port Royal, (now Annapolis,) where long and bitter lamentations, after the Indian fashion, were held over the embalmed remains by his bereaved widow, his father and mother, and at length by the whole body of his tribe.

In the spring, the corpse of Panounias was borne stealthily away by night in a solitary canoe, to be buried on a lone sandy islet, near the stormy Cape Sable. The situation of this *Island of the Dead* was known only to the *Aoutmoins*, or sorcerers of the tribe, and by them sacredly concealed, in order that the repose of their departed warriors might never be disturbed by enemy or stranger. In this wierd, grewsome island, desolated by the winds, and resounding with the roar of an ever tempestuous sea, Panounias lies asleep — dreaming, it may be, of the blissful voyage when, with his dusky bride, he guided the Frenchmen along our New England coast, and pointed out to Champlain and Champdoré, the "*isles asses hautes.*"

But Panounias died not unsung nor unavenged. Membertou, the Sagamo of the Souriquois, summoned all his braves to the war-path, and, the next summer, made a determined assault upon the murderers at Saco. Many of the Armouchiquois fell, and much blood was shed, before Membertou's vengeance was satiated. L'Escarbot, who witnessed the departure of the avenging expedition from Port Royal, in 1607, and also its triumphant return, composed a poem upon its achievements, which is — such as it is — the first epic ever composed in North America.[1]

[1] It is to be found in "Les Muses de la Nouvelle France," Paris 1612.

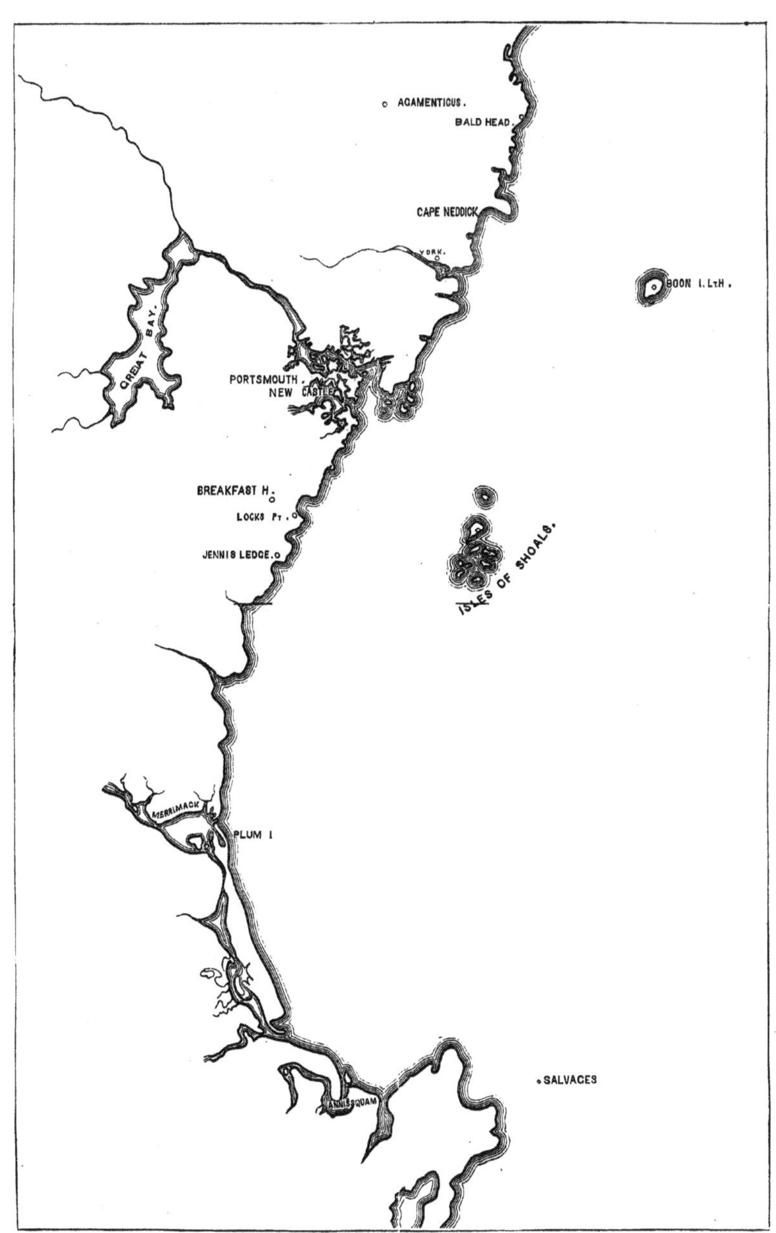

COÁST LINE MAP.

CHAPTER II.

FOR a number of years after the French abandoned this attempt at the colonization of New England, our coasts remained, in the language of Captain Smith, "*a rockie, barren, desolate desart.*" The Popham colony at Sagadehoc had vanished, and seven years later, we are told, "there was not one Christian in all the land."

But the teeming waters of the Gulf of Maine were still frequented by considerable fleets of fishing vessels during the summer season. Among others, came up from Virginia the renowned Sir Samuel Argal. His first acquaintance with these waters was made in 1610, when he and a consort, under Sir George Somers, were driven by a tempest far out of their course, into the mouth of the Penobscot River.

It was during the previous year (1609), that Sir George Somers, being on a voyage from England with emigrants and stores for the perishing colony of Virginia, was wrecked on the Bermuda Islands — the "*still vexed Bermoothes*" of Shakespeare — the fabled island of ambergris, and pearls and gems — the beautiful realm of sprite and fairy; of "sounds and sweet airs that give delight, but hurt not —" where the great Master has laid the scene of the "Tempest."

Upon this island, Sir George built a "new cedar ship," though without any "iron at all, but one bolt in her keele," and embarking in her, succeeded next year in reaching Jamestown, where he found the colony in sore distress for lack of provisions. Sir George at once volunteered, accompanied by Sir Samuel Argal, to make a voyage back to the Bermudas in quest of supplies. Sir George's pinnace was named the "Patience" — the same cedar ship he had built at Bermuda.

For days and weeks did the frail barks encounter "a most terrible and vehement storm, which was a taile of the West India Horacano," as though the magic wand of Prospero had again for some wise purpose put the "wild waters in a roar." But the "Patience" had been constructed in an enchanted isle, and seemed to possess a charmed life. She and her consort, named the "Discovery," bore away at last towards the north, and took refuge among the islands along the coast of Maine,

> "Not a hair blemished,
> But fresher than before."

The vessels then became separated, — the "Patience" at length reaching her destination at the Bermudas, while Argal spent the whole summer in cruising and fishing up and down the coast of Maine. The account of his voyages to and fro the gulf, to be found in *Purchas' Pilgrims*, puts it out of doubt, that the intrepid Sir Samuel Argal must have frequently, during that summer, made a harbor at the Isles of Shoals. He returned to Virginia, at the close of the season, in good safety, heavily freighted with fish.

Sir Samuel's experience, acquired in this enforced voyage to New England, was to have an important influence upon her future history. In 1613, he renewed his visit to our coast, as a pilot and convoy to a fleet of ten or eleven fishing vessels, which set out from Virginia, according to their yearly custom, for our waters. On the arrival of the squadron at Pemaquid, he received from the Indians the startling intelligence, that the French were again making encroachments upon English territory, by the recent settlement of the Jesuits at *Saint Sauveur* on *Mount Desert.* Argal at once fell upon that settlement, destroyed the buildings in progress of erection, killed one of the Jesuit priests, named Gilbert du Thet, shipped away to France a portion of the prisoners and carried off the remainder to Jamestown. The same summer, under the instructions of the Governor of Virginia, he returned to Acadia, and destroyed all the French settlements at St. Croix and Port Royal, with such thoroughness, indeed, that "he even caused the names of de Monts and other captains, and the fleurs de lys, to be effaced with pick and chisel from the massive stone at Port Royal, on which they had been engraved." A few of the homeless French took refuge in the friendly wigwams of the Micmac tribes, but their national power was extinguished in Acadia for many years.[1]

Thus was New England again rescued from an impending French invasion; the first time by the capricious indifference of de Monts and Champlain; the second time, if we may indulge the fancy, by the friendly help of the mighty magician of the Bermudas. His prophetic spirit, perhaps, descried far away in the north the peril to which New England was exposed, and in his own deep counsel he evoked the "horicano," which drove her champion, Sir Samuel Argal, into the

[1] For authorities concerning the story of Sir Samuel Argal, see Relations des Jesuits (Quebec Ed.) p. 46, *et seq.*; Smith's Gen. Hist., Vol. II., pp. 6–112, *et seq.*; Murdock's Hist. of Nova Scotia, vol. I., p. 55, *et seq.*; Champlain's Voyages; Purchas his Pilgrims, pp. 1733, 1734, *et seq.*

waters of the Gulf of Maine, in season for her protection. Is not Prospero's motive, indeed, suggested in his reply to his daughter?

"*Miranda.* And now, I pray you, sir,
(For still 'tis beating in my mind) your reasons
For raising this sea-storm?
"*Prospero.* Know thus far forth —
By accident, most strange, bountiful Fortune
(Now my dear lady) hath mine enemies
Brought to that shore; and by my prescience
I find my zenith doth depend upon
A most auspicious star; whose influence
If now I court not, but omit, my fortunes
Will ever after droop.— Here cease more questions."

CHAPTER III.

IT was in the following year, 1614, that the Isles of Shoals were visited by another of the marvellous men of that heroic age — *Captain John Smith.*

He came out in command of two London ships, upon a fishing and trading voyage, and arrived at Monhegan Island in April 1614.

"Our plot was," writes the captain, "there to take whales, and also to make trials of a mine of gold and copper; if these failed, fish and furs were then our refuge to make ourselves sauers howsoever; we found this whale fishing a costly conclusion; we saw many, and spent much time in chasing them, but could not kill any, they being a kind of *Jubartes*, and not the whale that yields fins and oil, as we expected; for our gold, it was rather the master's device to get a voyage that projected it, than any knowledge he had at all of any such matter." Meantime, while the crew fished, Smith and eight sailors in a small pinnace, very much after the manner of his great predecessor, Champlain, ranged the whole New England coast as far as Cape Cod, and trucked successfully with the natives for peltries. Returning thence to his vessels about Monhegan, he sailed for home on the 14th of July.

Shortly after his arrival in England, he published his interesting account of our coast, which, by the leave of Prince Charles, he named *New England*, and accompanied it with the chart, an exact copy of which is prefixed to this chapter.

"Among the remarkablest Isles and mountains for landmarks," writes Capt. Smith in his "Description of New England," "are Smiths Isles, a heape together, none neare them, against Accominticus."

The islands referred to were the present Isles of Shoals. The great navigator chose, out of his vast discoveries in the New World, these wild and picturesque rocks to perpetuate his name, and, as we shall hereafter see, selected the headland and islands in view to the south, to keep the world in memory of some of his most gallant achievements.

A few years after his return to London, the numerous patentees of New England formed a scheme to divide up its territory into twenty parts, and cast lots among themselves for the different portions. "But no lot for me," writes the Captain sorrowfully, "but Smiths Isles, which are a many of barren rocks, the most overgrowne with such shrubs and sharp whins you can hardly pass them, without either grass or wood, but three or four short shrubby old cedars."

We thus perceive, that Admiral John Smith was not only the first to *name* these Islets, but also that he claimed to be Lord and Proprietor of them, until the scheme of raffling for New England was abandoned.

We pause for a moment over the memory of the gallant Captain, New England's earliest and best friend, who by his untiring zeal, probably contributed more than any other man to the settlement of her shores and islands.

His career was as marvellous as the fabled exploits of Sir Launcelot, in quest of the San Graal, or of Sir Roland, who winded his horn at Roncesvalles. Stung with a spirit of adventure, he left his home with ten shillings in his pocket, while yet a boy, and served several years in the wars of the Low Countries. On his return to Scotland, he narrowly escaped death in the wreck of his ship on Holy Isle, near Berwick. Then, for a time, he retired into the midst of a dense forest, and dwelt "in a secluded pavillion, built of boughs," where he devoted himself to the study of Marcus Aurelius and Macchiavelli's "Art of War." When his restless spirit had wearied of a hermit's life, he returned to the continent, and after encountering many perils, reached Marseilles, where he embarked for Italy.

On this voyage, the ship fell into bad weather, and in the hope of appeasing the wrath of Neptune, the superstitious sailors threw our unfortunate hero into the Mediterranean. Again, however, he escaped death, having been picked up by a couple of ships from Britanny, with whom he enlisted, and shortly afterwards engaged, in their service, in a bloody but victorious fight with a Venetian argosy. After that, he made his way into Hungary, and took service under the German Emperor, in his wars against the Turk. Splendid feats of valor did he there perform; his fame resounded over that far quarter of the world. But at last, he fell prisoner to the Paynim, and was carried captive into the Steppes of Crym-Tartary. Escaping thence, he made his way back to Europe, on foot; he carried his free lance into the wars of Africa; ere long, we find him again at sea, where, with his single ship, he fought triumphantly against a pair of Spanish men-of-war, and returned with his prizes to England. Having thus performed, in all the three quarters of the known earth, such "doughty deeds of high emprise," as would put to shame the very knights of the Round Table, though with such modesty, says one of his eulogists, that he deemed all his exploits no more than "to go to bed or drink," the redoubtable captain entered upon his career in the New World. His valorous deeds in Virginia, of which plantation he was one of the earliest and most efficient promoters, are familiar to all Americans, and his rescue from Powhattan by the love-stricken Pochahontas is one of the staples of American story.

Some years after, in 1614, he came over to New England and landed upon "*Smiths Isles*," now the "*Isles of Shoals*." Only two years later, having undertaken another voyage hitherward, he was captured by a squadron of French pirates, and for a long time was *compelled*, as he assures us, to assist them in many a buccaneering enterprise on the high seas, until at last, in the midst of a terrible tempest in the Bay of Biscay, he deserted them in an open boat, and made good his escape all alone to Rochelle, while the pirate ship he had abandoned, was totally wrecked in the storm, and nearly all her crew perished. Then he returned to England, where he had long been given up for dead, and there he wrote the strange story of his life, discoveries, and exploits, as he expresses it, "*with his own hand.*"

CHAPTER IV.

WE should hardly have felt justified in sketching here, even thus briefly, the strange adventures of this last of the Paladins and Lord of the Shoals, had not our hero seen fit to record some of the most gallant and stirring incidents in his career upon the very headland and rocks within view from his own Islets.

During the wars in Hungary, where Smith's sword, as we have seen, played so bright a part, it chanced that the town of Regall was besieged by the Christian army, and long time stoutly defended by the Moslem. At length, when the siege had become tedious and monotonous, one Lord Turbashaw, in the words of the chronicle, "to delight the ladies of Regall, who did long to see some court-like pastime, did defie any captain in the German army to combat with him for his head." The gallant Captain Smith, though but a small, slight man, accepted the Turk's challenge.

"Truce being made for that time," continues the chronicle, "the Rampiers all beset with fair dames and men in arms, the Christians in Battalio, Turbashaw, with a noise of Howboyes, entered the field well mounted and armed; on his shoulders were fixed a pair of great wings, compacted of eagle feathers, within a ridge of silver, richly garnished with gold and precious stones; a Janizary before him, bearing his lance, on each side another leading his horse; where long he stayed not, ere Smith, with a noise of trumpets, only a page bearing his lance, passing by him with a courteous salute, took his ground with such good success, that at the sound of the charge, he passed the Turke thorow the sight of his beaver, face, head, and all, that he fell dead to the ground, where alighting and unbracing his helmet he cut off his head, and the Turkes tooke his body, and so he returned without any hurt at all."

The next day, "*a vowed friend*" of the slain Turbashaw, named Grualgo, "*enraged with madnesse,*" sent Smith a "*particular challenge to regaine his friend's head, or lose his own.*" Suffice it to say, the defiance was accepted, the tournament was held, and the brave little captain was rewarded with a second Paynim head, that of the grim Grualgo.

And now Smith, elated with his successes, sent back a cartel to the ladies of Regall, "*that he was not so much enamored of their two champions' heads,*" but that if any Turk would come to the lists to redeem them, such Turk might carry back Smith's head also, "*if he could winne it.*"

Upon this, still a *third champion* of Turkish beauty and chivalry entered the lists. He saw no less than the stout, stark, Bonny Mulgro himself. We may be sure, the captain's heart rejoiced to encounter the infidel bravo. At it they went, and after a desperate conflict, the head of that truculent Moslem was added to those of Turbashaw and Grualgo.

These exploits soon reached the ears of the German Emperor, and in guerdon of Smith's bravery he granted him, by patent under his imperial hand and seal, "*Three Turks heads in a shield, for his coat of arms.*" Smith ever after bore these arms, and was thus constantly reminded of the exploits by which he had won them. Accordingly, when in 1614, he came out to the Isles of Shoals, one of the first names he conferred upon the neighboring localities, was that of the *Three Turks' Heads*, which he gave to the three rocky islets at the head of Cape Ann, in view from the Shoals, of a clear day.

In these Turkish wars, however, fortune at last played false with the Christians. At the battle of Rottenton, the army of the latter was routed, and the intrepid captain was taken prisoner, and sold as a slave to the Bashaw Bogall. The Bashaw, who chanced to be at the time enamored of the fair Princess Charatza Tragabigzanda, sent him in chains to Constantinople, as a rich present to his mistress; arrived, there, however, the captain found exceeding favor in the eyes of the Oriental beauty. His chains were speedily stricken off, and in order to remove him from danger, she sent him to the care of her brother, the Prince of Nalbrits, a province in Crym-Tartary, on the Black Sea. But the brother, resenting his sister's affection for the Christian slave, treated him so harshly, that, at last, Smith "beat out the Timur's brains with a threshing bat," and donning the slain man's apparel, escaped on foot, and after infinite perils and fatigues, into Europe.

But the gallant captain never could forget the devotion of the lovely Princess Tragabigzanda. And upon his arrival, many years after, at the Isles of Shoals, while he named, as we have stated, the rocks at the point of Cape Ann, the *Three Turks'*

Heads, he conferred upon the Cape itself, the cherished name of *Cape Tragabigzanda*.

Captain Smith, afterwards appointed Admiral of New England, never beheld his beloved Islands after his visit of 1614. Even the names he conferred upon our coast were doomed to be soon forgotten. Cape Tragabigzanda in a few years became Cape Ann; the "*Three Turks' Heads*" were translated into the "*Salvages*," and in 1623, the rightful appellation of "*Smith's Isles*" was supplanted among the English, by that of the "*Isles of Shoals*"—the last English writer to stand by the honest name, being Edward Winslow, of New Plymouth, who, under date of 1623, describes the plantation, begun that year at the Piscataqua, by David Thompson, as being "near Smith's Isles."

The more constant Dutch, however, maintained their allegiance to the admiral for half a century later. On the quaint chart of "Novi Belgii" contained in Montanus' "Nieuwe onbekende Weereld," published at Amsterdam in 1671, and translated by John Ogleby, Cape Ann is still called *Cape Tragabigzanda*; the three rocks, at its point, the *3 Turcks hoofden*, and the Isles of Shoals, "*Smit's Eylant.*" As applied to the rocks themselves, the name of John Smith has long since passed into oblivion, unless, as we may fondly hope, it lingers in the little cove at the south-west angle of Appledore, which is still called *Smith's Cove.*

Captain Smith died in London, in 1631, at the age of 52, and was buried there in St. Sepulchre's Church. Upon his monument is cut the following inscription: —

"To the living memory of his deceased friend, Capt. John Smith, some time Governor of Virginia and Admiral of New England, who departed this life the 21st of June, 1631.

ACCORDIAMUS, VINCERE EST VIVERE.

Here lies one conquered, that hath conquered kings,
Subdued large territories, and done things
Which to the world impossible would seem,
But that the truth is held in more esteem.
Shall I report his former service done,
In honor of his God and Christendom?
How that he did divide from Pagans three
Their heads and lives, types of his chivalry;
For which great service, in that climate done,
Brave Sigismundus (King of Hungarion)
Did give him, as a coat of arms to wear
Those conquered heads, got by his sword and spear?
Or shall I tell of his adventures, since
Done in Virginia, that large continent?
How that he subdued kings unto his yoke,
And made those heathen flee as wind doth smoke;
And made their land, being of so large a station
A habitation for our Christian nation,
Where God is glorified, their wants supplied,
Which, for necessaries, might have died?
But what avails his conquest, now he lies
Interr'd in earth, a prey to worms and flies?

O may his soul in sweet Elysium sleep,
Until the Keeper, that all souls doth keep,
Return to judgment; and that after thence,
With angels he may have his recompence."[1]

A neat marble monument, erected some years ago, on the southerly summit of Star Island by several public-spirited citizens of New Hampshire, puts the summer visitor in mind of the departed hero and of his long and intimate connection with these, his "heape of rocks, none neare them against Accominticus."

[1] Jesse's Hist. of London.

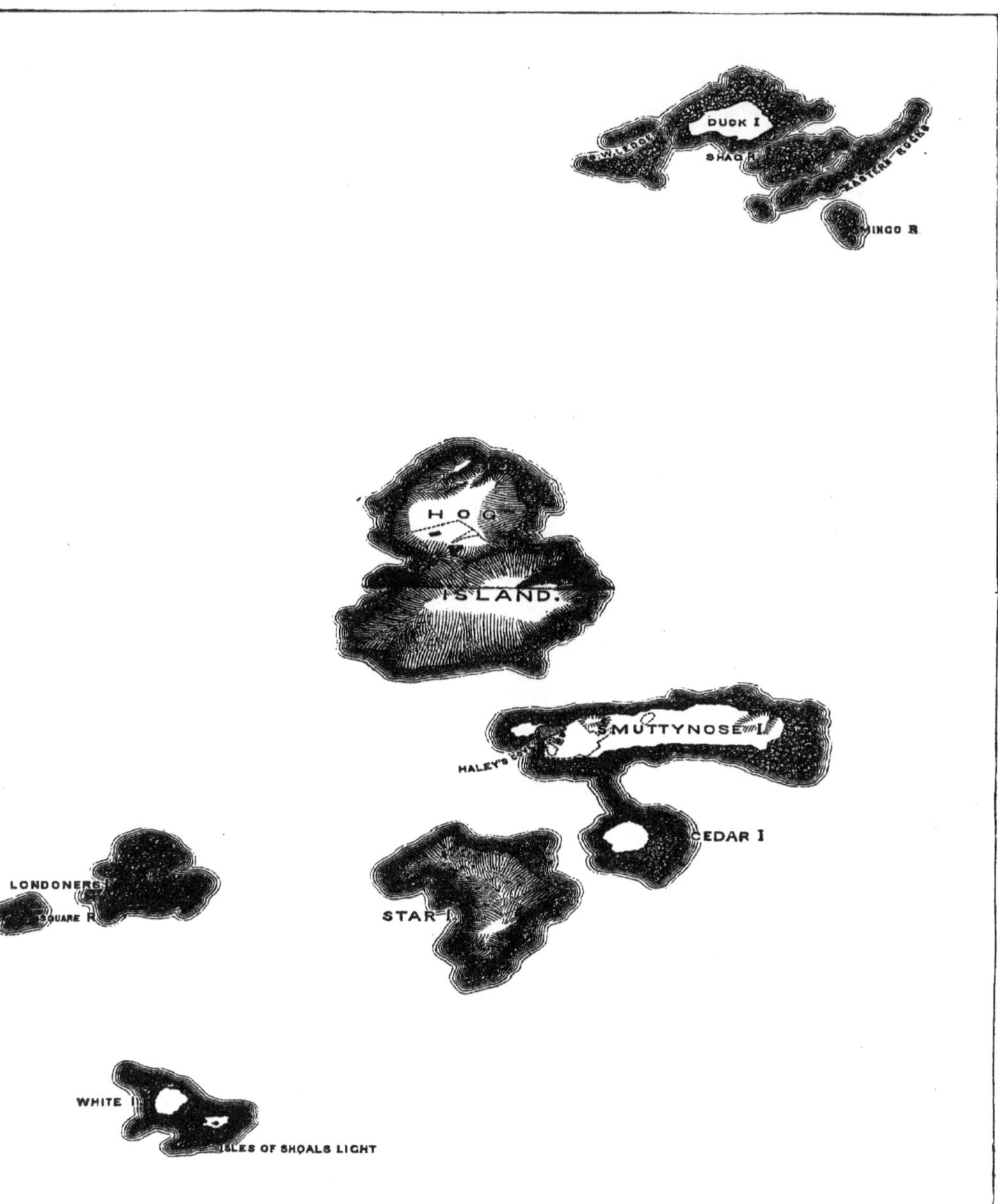

THE ISLES OF SHOALS.

CHAPTER V.

SOME five years after the memorable expedition of Admiral John Smith to New England, there is evidence,[1] that our coasts were visited, about 1619, by those two great men, who subsequently became the fathers and founders of the Provinces of New Hampshire and Maine. John Mason, then Governor of New Foundland, and Sir Ferdinando Gorges made, that summer, it is said, a cruise of discovery along the New England coast, and on their return to London; presented a report of their voyage to the King.

That report is not now extant, but from the general course of their voyage, as well as the strong interest both those gentlemen afterward took in the Isles of Shoals, there is reason to believe that they failed not to pay them a visit.

Upon the return of these renowned men to Eng-

[1] Early documents relating to Maine, collected by Folsom.

land, evidently pleased with the aspect of the country they had visited, Gorges, who had been for several years a merchant adventurer to our coasts, set about the colonization of New England with renewed ardor. Mason, upon the termination of his office in New Foundland, entered into his friend's project with equal zeal. Gorges, the next year, 1620, obtained from His Majesty a new and enlarged patent for the extensive territory between the 40th and 48th parallels of latitude, incorporating forty noblemen, knights, and gentlemen, under the title of "The Council established at Plymouth in the County of Devon, for planting, ruling and governing New England in America." This charter is the foundation of the numerous subsequent patents by which New England was first parcelled out, and its settlements and colonies located and limited.[1]

Shortly after this great charter of New England had passed the seals, Mason and Gorges, "the projectors and prosecutors of still greater designs," procured of the Plymouth Council, August 10th, 1622, a sub-patent, for all the country between the Merrimac and the Sagadahock, under the title of the Province of Maine.[2] It was under this sub-patent, that the first

[1] Gorges' Brief Narrative, p. 32.

[2] 1 New Hamp. Prov. Pap., p. 10.

settlements in New Hampshire and Maine were made.

The next year, 1623, the Council of Plymouth, having projected the establishment of a permanent general government over all New England, sent out Robert Gorges, son of Sir Ferdinando, "an active, enterprising genius, and a brilliant officer in the late Venetian war," as Governor-in-Chief of the country. His council was to consist, among others, of Christopher Levett, who had already arrived in New England, and was now visiting David Thompson, at Odiorne's Point on the coast of New Hampshire.

The reign of Governor Robert Gorges was, however, very brief. He returned to England the next year, and the attempt to establish any general government over New England was for the time abandoned. The reason of this sudden change of policy, on the part of the Grand Council of Plymouth, is worthy a moment's attention, on account of its important political significance, as well as the influence our poor fishermen exercised in the matter.

The Council, enjoying, by the terms of their charter,[1] a monopoly of the fisheries in the "adjoining seas" of

[1] See the Charter, 1 Hazard, State Pap., p. 103.

New England, with a right to "take and surprise" any ships, that presumed to visit the said seas, "unless it be with the license of said Council, under the common seal," promulgated an order, shortly after their incorporation, imposing a charge of five pounds sterling upon every thirty tons of shipping engaged in the American fisheries, as the cost of such necessary license.[1] The ostensible purpose of this license system was, by a careful scrutiny into the character and previous conduct of all applicants, to protect the poor American savages from the cruelties and frauds practiced on them by disorderly fishermen.[2] It was urged "that the mischiefs already sustained from these disorderly persons are inhuman and intolerable. That, in their manners and behaviour, they are worse than the very savages, openly abusing their women, teaching their men to drink drunk, to swear and blaspheme the name of God, and in their drunken humor to fall together by the ears, thereby giving them occasion to seek revenge. . Besides that, they cozen and abuse the savages in trading and trafficking, selling them salt covered with butter, instead of so much butter, and the like cozenages and deceits, whereby to bring the planters and

[1] 2 Smith's Gen. Hist., p. 263.

[2] Gorges' Brief Nar., p. 38.

all the nation into contempt and disgrace."[1] But the *real* design of the order, notwithstanding this specious pretext, was to raise a revenue for the use of the Grand Council itself, and it was therefore met at the outset with loud complaints from the fishermen, who had for so many years enjoyed the absolute freedom of the New England seas.

The Commons of England, who were just at that time warming up to that determined struggle with the royal prerogative, which culminated by-and-by in the Great Rebellion, seized eagerly upon the present opportunity, to make a stand against King James. Parliament convened in June, 1621, and proceeded at once to the examination of the national grievances. In the very head and front of them all, they set the odious fishery monopoly of the Council of Plymouth. The Commons then summoned Sir Ferdinando Gorges to defend the patent.

"The whole House being dissolved into a committee," writes Gorges, "Sir Edward Coke being in the chair, I was called for to the bar, where after some space, it pleased him to tell me, that the House understood, that there was a patent granted to me and divers other noble persons therein nominated, for the estab-

[1] Gorges' Brief Nar., p. 38.

lishing of a colony in New England. This (as it seems) was a grievance of the Commonwealth, and so complained of, in respect of many particulars therein contained, contrary to the laws and privileges of the subjects, as also that it was a monopoly."[1]

Sir Ferdinando defended the charter at the bar of the House with pertinacity and skill, but the Commons, under the leadership of Coke, Selden, and Pym, stood resolute against this and all other monopolies, in defiance of the overbearing and supercilious reproofs of King James.

At length, in the winter of 1622, despairing of any concession on the part of the House, the King dissolved the Parliament in a rage, and committed Sir Edward Coke, Selden, Pym and others to prison.[2]

The Commons had thus failed in their effort to vacate the great charter of New England, the fishing monopoly still remained legally in the hands of the patentees, and the next spring, (1623), the bolder of their number determined to enforce it. They sent out, accordingly, Robert Gorges as Governor, and Frances West as Admiral, to make their monopoly effectual.

But the confidence of many of the patentees and

[1] Gorges' Brief Nar., p. 34.

[2] 5 Hume, p. 133.

adventurers in the stability of their monopoly had been shaken by the commotion. Many of them withdrew altogether from New England affairs; the fishermen from whom the revenue was to be derived, "grew so discontented," says Capt. Smith, "that few or none would goe,"[1] and as to the few who did go, Admiral West found it as difficult to collect fines of them, as of the cod-fish in the ocean. Hence the Grand Council of Plymouth, deeming it the part of prudence to yield for a time to the popular storm, withdrew their Governor and Admiral from New England, a few months after their arrival, and abandoned their project until a more favorable season.

The scheme, however, of a General Governor and a State religion for all New England was a deeply cherished one with the Grand Council of Plymouth until its dissolution, and was persisted in by its leading spirits, Sir Ferdinando Gorges and Capt. John Mason, to the last. The warrant for the commission to Captain Mason, as Vice-Admiral of New England, had actually passed the seals at the time of his decease in 1635.[2] But for his death at that time, it is altogether probable that a renewed effort to found a general government under Gorges and Mason would have

[1] Smith's Gen. Hist., p. 263.

[2] Catal. of Early Doc. relating to Maine, p. 10.

been speedily made. Winthrop seems to have feared such an attempt. He says: "The last winter Capt. Mason died. He was the chief mover in all the attempts against us, and was to have sent the General Governor, and for this end was providing shipping; but the Lord, in mercy, taking him away, all the business fell on sleep."[1]

But the germ of popular liberty implanted in the hearts of the English people, in part by the rude fishermen of the Gulf of Maine, large numbers of whom made their stages at the Isles of Shoals, was not destroyed. Many years after, it ripened into the great Rebellion, which drenched the United Kingdom in blood, and brought the sacred person of his Majesty to the scaffold.

[1] Winthrop, Vol. I., p. 187.

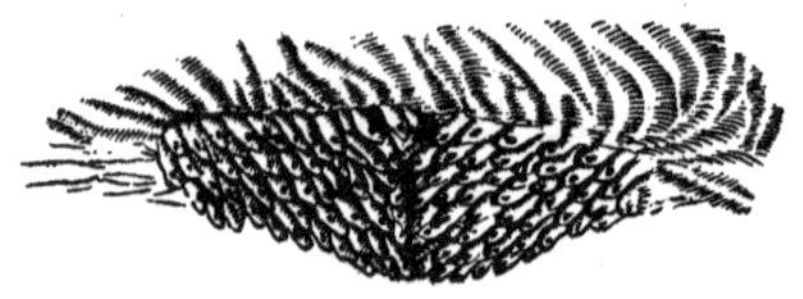

CHAPTER VI.

AMONG the chief adherents of the Gorges family, in this futile attempt to found a general government for New England, was Capt. Christopher Levett, "his Majesty's Woodward of Somersetshire, and one of the Council of New England," and as he describes himself, "an ancient traveller by sea."

Capt. Levett, having procured for himself, the previous year, a patent for six thousand acres of land, to be located at his own pleasure upon the vacant territory of New England,[1] set sail from England in the spring of 1623, in a vessel bound for the Isles of Shoals, and arrived there in the early summer. He describes the group as follows:[2]

"The first place I set my foot upon in New England was the Isles of Shoulds, being islands in the sea, about two leagues from the main.

[1] English Calendar of State Papers, Colonial, p. 45.

[2] Levett's Voyage, 2 Maine Hist. Coll., p. 72.

"Upon these islands I neither could see one good timber tree, nor so much ground as to make a garden.

"The place is found to be a good fishing place for six ships, but more cannot well be there, for want of convenient stage room, as this year's experience hath proved.

"The harbor is but indifferent good. Upon these islands are no savages at all."

Shortly afterward, Capt. Levett crossed over to the plantation just begun by David Thompson at Odiorne's Point, (called by Levett, Pannaway,) the first settlement on the mainland of New Hampshire. Here he remained about a month, until the arrival of Governor Robert Gorges, from whom Levett learned that he had been appointed a Councillor to the new Government of New England.

Levett was a staunch churchman, as were also his friends, the Governor and Admiral West; and in furtherance of the scheme to establish a general government over New England, he seems to have been specially charged with the founding of the Episcopal church there. The first step to that end, according to church usages, was the creation of some *city*, with all the pomp and paraphernalia of city government, as a suitable Episcopal see; and accordingly Captain Levett, for the purpose of selecting the most favorable site for the establishment of the projected metropolis, made a cruise in two boats, with all his company, along the coast of Maine, as far as Cape Manwagan, now Boothbay, putting in on the voyage at a place called "Quack," which was at that time under the government of an Indian sagamore, named "Cogawesco."

The peninsula of Quack, (now called Portland), seemed in the captain's eyes a preferable site for his projected plantation, to any other he had visited; and, accordingly, after sailing as far east as Boothbay, he resolved to return and settle there; especially because, as Levett writes, "Cogawesco, the sagamore of Casco and Quack, told me if I would set down at either of those places, I should be very welcome."

"The next day," the captain continues, "the wind came fair, and I sailed to Quack or York, with the King, Queen and Prince, bow and arrows, dog and kettle in my boat, his noble attendance rowing by us in their canoe."

"And thus," he concludes, "after many dangers, much labor, and great charge, I have obtained a place of habitation in New England, where I have built a house and fortified it in a reasonable good fashion, strong enough against such enemies as are those savage people."

Towards the close of the summer, Levett made ready to return into England, in furtherance of his enterprise, leaving ten of his men in his garrison house at Quack, until his proposed return the next year. He was visited before his departure by the great sagamores of the country, who entreated him to still remain among them.

"They asked me," writes Levett, "why I would be gone out of their country? I was glad to tell them my wife would not come thither, except I did fetch her; they bid a pox on her hounds (a phrase they have learned and do use when they curse), and wished me to beat her; I told them no, for then our God would be angry; then they run out upon her with evil terms, and wished me to let her alone and take another. I told them our God would be more angry for that. Again they bid me beat her, repeating it often and very angerly, but I answered no, that was not the English fashion. Then they told me that I and my wife and children with all my friends should be heartily welcome into that country, at any time, yea, a hundredth thousand times, yea, *mouchicke, mouchicke*, which is a word of weight."

"And Somerset told me that his son, (who was born

whilst I was in the country, and whom he would needs have me to name,) and mine would be brothers, and that there should be *mouchicke legamatch* (that is friendship) between them, until *Tanto* carried them to his wigwam (that is, until they died)."[1]

Despite these moving arguments and entreaties, Captain Levett sailed for England in the fall of 1623, and learning on his arrival that the scheme of the Grand Council of Plymouth to establish a general civil and religious government over New England, had been reluctantly abandoned, and their Governor and Admiral recalled, he gave over his design of returning to Quack for several years, and his fortified habitation at that place was no doubt deserted by its garrison.

Governor Robert Gorges died in 1624, shortly after his return to England. Captain Levett enlisted in the Royal Navy, where he seems to have served with distinction for several years. In 1628, it was believed, now that peace was restored to England, the time was auspicious for a renewal of the Grand Council's design to establish Episcopacy in New England.

Captain Levett threw up his commission in the navy, and in that year was appointed by Royal Commission Governor of New England; and he was authorized by his majesty's letters to raise large contributions

[1] 2 Maine Hist. Col., p. 72.

and benevolences in the County and City of York, England, for the purpose of founding a capital and episcopal seat, to be named York, upon the present site of Portland.[1] We can hardly conjecture what might have been the result of the Captain's efforts, both in a political and religious point of view, had he not been removed by death, before he had gathered the fruits of his ambitious zeal.

[1] Col. of State Papers, Colonial.

CHAPTER VII.

CAPTAIN Levett's brief description of the Shoals illustrates the importance of that station, even so early as 1623. When we consider, that each of the six fishing vessels at the Islands, while he was there, carried at least fifty men, as he informs us was the custom, and that the shores were inconveniently crowded with fishing stages, we perceive that, even before the first settlement of the mainland, our group of Islets was already the scene of a busier activity, than any other spot in New England, north of New Plymouth.

It was the usual course of the fishery, in those days, for about one-third of each crew to live ashore, and attend to the drying and curing of the catch, while the remainder, in their pinnace and shallops, cruised about the neighboring ocean in quest of mackerel or cod. Shelter for the large number of shoremen out of these six ships would, of course, be essential, and numerous cabins, however rude, must have already been built for their accommodation.

The "fishing stages," which Capt. Levett speaks of, were floating platforms, projecting from the margin of the Islands into the waters of the harbor, and the rocks at the shore end were roofed over by an open shed, used for the splitting and salting of the fish, which were afterwards dried upon the flakes in the rear. These structures, which are still used in Newfoundland, were somewhat expensive, and convenient stage-room for their erection upon the generally steep shores of the Islands was difficult to obtain. For many years, on this account, the stage-room and fishing stages formed the most valued part of the islanders' property. The circumstance that the harbor was inconveniently crowded with stages at the time of Capt. Levett's visit, conveys a lively idea of the extent of business already transacted there.

The Islands enjoyed, indeed, singular advantages for the prosecution of the fisheries.

"In March, April, May and half June," says the Lord of the Isles, in his own quaint language, "here is cod in abundance. The salvages compare the store in the sea with the hairs upon their heads, and surely there are an incredible abundance of them upon the coast. Then, too, young boies and girles, salvages or any other, be they never such *idles*, may turne, carry, or return a fish, without either shame or any great pain. He is very idle, that is past twelve years of age, and cannot do so much, and she is very old, that cannot spin a threede to make engins to catch a fish.

"He is a very bad fisher, that cannot kill in one day with his hook and line one, two, or three hundred cods. And is it not pretty sport to pull up two pence, six pence, and twelve pence, as fast as you can hale and veare a line? And what sport doth yield a more pleasing content and less hurt or charge, than angling with a hook, and crossing the sweete Ayre from Ile to Ile over the silent streams of a calm sea? wherein the most curious may find pleasure, profit and content."[1]

The codfish caught in the seas about the Islands were larger and finer than those brought from the Banks of Newfoundland, "six or seven making a quintal, whereas they have fifteen of the latter of the same weight."[2] And besides the cod, "there is," continues old William Wood, "all manner of other fish, as followeth: —

"The king of waters, the sea shouldering Whale,
The snuffing Grampus, with the oily Seale,
The storm-presaging Porpus, Herring-Hogge,
Line shearing Sharke, the Catfish, and Sea Dogge,

[1] 2 Smith's Gen. Hist., pp. 188, 201.
[2] Wood's New England Prospect, p. 35.

The scale-fenc'd Sturgeon, cony-mouthed Hollibut,
The flounsing Sammon, Codfish, Greedigut,
Cole, Haddocke, Haicke, the Thornebacke, and the Scate,
Whose slimie outside makes him selde in date,
The stately Basse, old Neptune's fleeting post,
That tides it out and in from sea to coast,
Consorting Herrings, and the bony Shad,
Big bellied Alewives, Mackrills richly clad
With rainbow colors, the Frostfish and the Smelt
As good as ever lady Gustus felt;
The spotted Lamprons, Eeles, the Lamperies,
That seeke fresh water brooks with Argus eyes;
These waterie villagers with thousands more,
Doe passe and repasse neare the verdant shore."(1)

In addition to all these advantages for the fisheries, the Isles of Shoals enjoyed in their climate a very marked advantage over other parts of the New England coast, in the curing of their fish for the market. The dryness and salubrity of their atmosphere, to which we have referred in the Introduction, enabled the fishermen to prepare by a process of alternate drying and sweating, without salt, the famous *dun* or *dumb* fish, which could not be rivalled elsewhere. The market price of these fish was three or four times that of the Poor John and Haberdine, made at Newfoundland. Within the present century, we find the Labrador cod selling in our market at $2.40 per quin-

[1] Wood's New England Prospect, p. 37.

tal, while the Shoals-cured dun-fish brought $8.00 per quintal.[1]

All these excellences of the Shoals, as a fishing station, continued to lure vessels thither every summer, in spite of the withdrawal of the direct patronage of the Patentees. But towards the close of the French and Spanish wars, Sir Ferdinando Gorges and John Mason, now discharged from military service, turned their attention once more to their cherished schemes of New England colonization. They had jointly, in 1622, as we have already stated, obtained a patent for all the territory between the Merrimack and Sagadehock, by the name of the Province of Maine, under which the first feeble efforts at a settlement of New Hampshire were made. In 1629, (Nov. 7,) Mason obtained, by Gorges' consent,[2] a separate patent of the lands between the Merrimack and the Piscataqua, under the name of New Hampshire. And ten days afterwards, Gorges and Mason took out, jointly, a patent for a tract of territory, situated far to the west, near Lake Champlain, which they christened "Laconia." This latter grant also authorized the patentees " to make chois of and take and possess for their

[1] Portsmouth Journal, May, 1822.

[2] Catalogue of Orig. Doc. relating to Maine, p. 86.

own use in any of the ports, harbors or creeks in New England, lying most commodious for their passage up into the great lakes, one thousand acres of land on the side or sides of such ports or rivers."[1]

It was under this Laconia patent, which embraced no part of New Hampshire, that the colonization of that Province at the mouth of the river was now actively pushed forward. The territory of Laconia itself was never explored by the patentees, and the only agent they ever sent in quest of it, returned baffled, with a "*non est inventa provincia.*" Gorges and Mason, however, immediately upon taking out the Laconia patent, proceeded, in pursuance of the original design, to transform it into a charter for a trading and exploring company, and, perhaps, under the above quoted clause, located its chief emporium in the New World on the banks of the Piscataqua. They took into their co-partnership several wealthy merchants of London, and (Nov. 3, 1631,)[2] procured a further grant to themselves and their associates of a considerable tract of land on both sides of the river, where, for several years, these undertakers, or merchant adventurers, carried

[1] N. H. Prov. Papers, p. 38.

[2] Catl. of Orig. Doc. relating to Maine, p. 37.

forward zealously an extensive traffic in peltries, lumber and fish.

The Isles of Shoals, being at that time, as we have seen, the resort of large numbers of fishing vessels, were important to the merchant adventurers in the prosecution of their business; we find, accordingly, that in the grant and confirmation of "*Pascataway*," made Nov. 3, 1631, to which we have referred, the entire group of the Shoals was conveyed to the Company of Laconia;[1] a magazine was established there, and intercourse was maintained between them and the emporium on the mainland for several years.

But the enterprise of the merchant adventurers of the Company of Laconia proved, on the whole, unprofitable, and was, at last, abandoned. In 1633, a division of the Company's estate on the northerly side of the Piscataqua river was made among the individual adventurers; but the Shoals, and the estate on the south side of the river, were expressly retained as common property, until another and final distribution of the assets in 1635; at which time, as neither Mason nor Gorges wished to surrender their entire interest in these valuable Islands, the group was divided between them precisely

[1] Catalogue of Doc. rel. to Maine, p. 37.

upon the line, which, with a brief interruption, has been maintained to the present day. Gorges took the northerly half, and carried it with him into his subsequent province of Maine, while John Mason took the southerly half and annexed it to his province of New Hampshire.[1] This circumstance accounts for the singular division of our petty "heape of rocks" between the two governments. And we have ventured to explain this part of their history at some detail, although conscious that few readers can be interested by it, for the reason that none of our authors, to our knowledge, have set these matters out in a clear light.

During the existence of the Company of Laconia, both the Islands and the main land had become peopled with considerable numbers of laborers of all sorts, and permanent buildings had been erected. This population had remained long enough to take root, and upon the withdrawal of the Laconia Company, they formed themselves into voluntary combinations, and laid the foundation of a new and independent State.

The Isles of Shoals, under the patronage of the Laconia adventurers, had gained considerably in population and business, their rateable property being equal

[1] Catalogue of Early Doc. rel. to Maine, p. 46.

to that of New Plymouth itself; no less than seventeen fishing ships from Europe having arrived there and at Richman's Island in the month of March, 1633–4.[1] Edward Johnson, in his History of New England, written not long after, truly describes the Isles of Shoals as having become, at that day, "a great place for fishing for our English nation."[2] Lechford, in his "Plaine Dealing," written a few years later, characterizes the group in very similar language.[3] The importance of this little cluster of bare rocks was now, indeed, generally recognized, as a chief fishing station in the Gulf of Maine.

[1] 1 Winthrop, p. 124.

[2] Johnson's New England, ch. 30.

[3] Plaine Dealing, p. 107.

CHAPTER VIII.

AMONG those who visited the Shoals at this early period must not be forgotten the great name of Richard Mather, the founder and progenitor of that "*decemvirate*" of Mathers, who exercised such an important influence over the early history of New England.

Richard Mather writes, in the diary of his voyage to New England, under date of August 14, 1635: —

"This evening by moonlight, about ten of-the-clock, we came to anchor at the Isles of Shoals, which are seven or eight islands and other great rocks, and there slept sweetly that night, until break of day."

In the morning, however, one of the most terrible easterly storms broke on the sea, that has ever been known in New England. "Whereby," continues Richard, "we were in as much danger as I think ever people were. For we lost in that morning three great anchors and cables; of which cables, one, having cost £50, never had been in any water before; two were broken by the violence of the waves, and the third cut by the seamen in extremity and distress, to save the ship and their and our lives. And when our cables and anchors were all lost, we had no outward means of deliverance, but by loosing sail, if so be we might get to the sea from amongst the islands and rocks where we anchored. But the Lord let us see that our sails could not save us neither; no more than our cables and anchors. For, by the force of the wind and rain, the sails were rent in sunder and split in pieces, as if they had been but rotten rags, so that of the foresail and spritsail there was scarce left so much as a hand breadth that was not rent in pieces and blown away into the sea. So that at this time, all hope that we should be saved, in regard of any outward appearance, was utterly taken away; and rather because we seemed to drive with full force of wind and rain directly upon a mighty rock, standing out in sight above the water; so that we did but continually wait, when we should hear and feel the doleful rushing and crashing of the ship upon the rock. In this extremity and appearance of death, as distress and destruction would suffer us, we cried unto the Lord, and he was pleased to have compassion and pity upon us; for by his over-ruling Providence and his own immediate good hand, he guided the ship past the rock, assuaged the violence of the sea and of the wind and rain, and gave us a little respite to fit the ship with other sails and sent us a fresh gale of wind, by which we went on that day toward Cape Ann. It was a day much to be remembered, because on that day the Lord granted us as wonderful a deliverance, as I think ever people had, out of as apparent danger, as I think ever people felt. I am sure our seamen confessed they never knew the like. The Lord so imprint the memory of it on our hearts, that we may be better for it, and be more careful to please him, and to walk uprightly before him, as long as we live; and I hope we shall not forget the passages of that morning until our dying day."[1]

"The mighty rock," past which the immediate good hand of Providence guided the James of Bristol on this fearful morning was probably White Island, the westernmost of the Isles of Shoals.[2]

The three great anchors, which Mather's ship then lost, still lie, no doubt, beneath the waters of the Shoals harbor; most interesting relics, could they be recovered, of the first generation of our Puritan Fathers, and particularly of one of the greatest families among them.

[1] Young's Chronicles, p. 473.

[2] Compare 1 Winthrop, p. 165.

The tempest in which she was caught was, perhaps, the most furious that ever visited these exposed Islands Nearly all the contemporaneous writers of New Eng land describe its violence with dismay. Says Morton, who witnessed it at New Plymouth: "It was such a mighty storm of wind and rain, as none now living in these parts, either English or Indian, had seen the like, being like unto those hurricanes or tuffins that writers mention to be in the Indies. It began in the morning a little before day, and grew not by degrees, but came with great violence in the beginning, to the great amazement of many; it blew down sundry houses and uncovered divers others; many vessels were lost at sea in it, and many more in extreme danger. It caused the sea to swell in some places to the southward of Plymouth, as that it arose to twenty feet right up and down, and made many of the Indians to climb into trees for safety. It blew down many hundred thousands of trees, turning up the stronger by the roots, and breaking the high pine trees and such like in the midst, and the tall young oak and walnut trees of good bigness were wound as withes by it, very strange and fearful to behold; the marks of it will remain this many years in those parts where it was forest. The moon suffered a great eclipse two nights after it."[1]

[1] Morton's Memorial, p. 112.

Winthrop adds, that such was the violence of the tempest at sea, that in Boston harbor there were two flood tides within two hours of each other.[1]

It was, probably, in this same great storm, that a house, belonging to a tailor, named Tucker, was swept away by the waves from the rocks on Haley's or Smuttynose Island, and carried entire to Cape Cod, where it was hauled ashore, and a box of linen, papers, etc., which was found in it, made known from whence it came. The family had barely time to escape before the house was washed into the sea.[2]

That same fearful morning, Anthony Thatcher and his cousin Avery, with their families, were wrecked upon one of the small islands at the head of Admiral John Smith's Cape Tragabigzanda, near the Three Turks' Heads and in view from the Shoals. Thatcher was a poor tailor, without education or practice in composition; yet his simple narrative of the catastrophe, by its pathos, its unaffected piety, its homely truth, cannot fail, we think, to interest the reader.

"I must turn my drowned pen and shaking hand," writes Thatcher, "to indite the story of such sad news, as never before this happened in New England.

"There was a league of perpetual friendship be-

[1] 1 Winthrop, p. 164.

[2] 7 Mass. Hist. Coll. p. 252.

tween my cousin Avery and myself, never to forsake each other to the death, but to be partakers of each other's misery or welfare, as also of habitation in the same place.

"We embarked at Ipswich, August 11, 1635, with our families and substance, bound for Marblehead, we being in all twenty-three souls, viz.: 11 in my cousin's family, 7 in mine, one Mr. Eliot, and 4 mariners. The next morning, having commended ourselves to God, with cheerful hearts we set sail. But before daylight, (of August 15), it pleased the Lord to send so mighty a storm, as the like was never known in New England. It was so furious that an anchor came home; whereupon the mariners let out more cable, which at last slipped away. Then our sailors knew not what to do; but we were driven before the wind and waves.

"My cousin and I perceived our danger, and solemnly recommended ourselves to God, the Lord both of earth and seas, expecting with every wave to be swallowed up and drenched in the deeps. And as my cousin, his wife, and my tender babes sat comforting and cheering one the other in the Lord against ghastly death, which every moment stared us in the face, and sat triumphing on each one's forehead, we were by the violence of the waves and fury of the winds (by the Lord's permission) lifted up upon a rock between two high rocks, yet all was one rock. The waves came furiously and violently over us and against us, but by reason of the rock's proportion, could not lift us off, but beat her all to pieces. Now consider of my misery, who beheld the ship broken, the water violently overwhelming us, my goods and provisions swimming in the seas, my friends almost drowned, mine own poor children so untimely before mine eyes drowned, and ready to be swallowed up and dashed to pieces against the rocks by the merciless waves, and myself ready to accompany them.

"But from the greatest to the least of us, there was not one screech or outcry made; but all, as silent sheep, were contentedly resolved to die together, lovingly, as since our acquaintance we had lived together friendly.

"Now as I was sitting in the cabin room door, with my body in the room, when lo! one of the sailors, by a wave being washed out of the pinnace, was gotten in again, and coming into the cabin room over my back, cried out: 'We are all cast away! The Lord have mercy upon us! I have been washed overboard into the sea, and am gotten in again.' His speeches made me look forth, and seeing how we were, I turned myself to and spake these words: 'O, cousin, it hath pleased God to cast us here between two rocks, the shore not far from us, for I saw the tops of trees when I looked forth.' Whereupon the master of the pinnace, looking up at the scuttle hole of the quarter deck, went out at it, but I never saw him afterwards. Then he that had been in the sea went out again by me and leaped overboard towards the rocks, whom afterwards also I could not see.

"My cousin thought I would have fled from him, and said unto me: 'O, cousin, leave us not; let us die together,' and reached forth his hand unto me. Then I, letting go my son Peter's hand, took him by the hand, and said: 'Cousin, I purpose it not; whither shall I go? I am willing and ready here to die with you and my poor children. God be merciful to us and receive us to himself!'

"Which words I had no sooner spoken, but by a mighty wave I was, with the piece of the bark, washed out upon part of the rock, where the wave left me almost drowned. But recovering my feet, I saw above me on the rock my daughter, Mary, to whom I had no sooner gotten, but my cousin, Avery, and his eldest son came to us, being all four of us washed out by one and the same wave. We called to those in the pinnace to come to us. My wife, seeing us there, was crept up into the scuttle of the quarter deck to come unto us. But presently came another wave, and dashing the pinnace all to pieces, carried my wife away in the scuttle, as she was, with the greater part of the quarter deck, unto the shore, where she was cast safely but something bruised. All the rest that were in the bark were drowned in the merciless seas. We four by that wave were clean swept away from off the rock also into the sea; the Lord, in one instant of time, disposing of fifteen souls of us, according to his good pleasure and will.

"As I was sliding off the rock into the sea, the Lord directed my toes into a joint in the rock's side, and also the tips of some of my fingers, by means whereof, the wave leaving me, I remained so, hanging on the rock, only my head above the water. By another wave I was washed away from the rock, and driven hither and thither in the seas a great while, and had many dashes against the rocks. At length, past hopes of life, and wearied in body and spirits, I even gave over to nature, and being ready to receive in the waters of death, I lifted up both my heart and hands to the God of Heaven, — for note, I had my senses remaining perfect with me all the time that I was under and in water; who at that instant lifted my head above the top of the water, so I might breathe without any hindrance by the waters. I stood bolt upright, as if I had stood upon my feet, but I felt no bottom, nor had any footing to stand upon but the waters.

"Suddenly I was overwhelmed with waters, and driven to and fro again, and at last I felt the ground with my right foot. I made haste to get out, and with safety crept to the dry shore, where, blessing God, I turned about to look for my children and friends, but saw neither, nor any part of the pinnace. But I saw my wife about a butt length from me, gotten to the shore.

"When we were come together, we went and sat down together under the bank. But fear of the seas roaring and our coldness would not suffer us there to remain. But we went up into the land and sat us down under a cedar tree, which the wind had thrown down, where we sat about an hour, almost dead with cold.

"Now came to my remembrance the time and manner, how and when I last saw and left my children and friends. One was severed from me sitting on the rock at my feet, the other three in the pinnace; my little babe (ah, poor Peter!) sitting in his sister Edith's arms, who, to the uttermost of her power, sheltered him from the waters; my poor William standing close unto them, all three of them looking ruefully on me on the rock, their very countenances calling unto me to help them. Oh, I yet see their cheeks, poor silent lambs, pleading pity and help at my hands!

"I and my wife were almost naked, both of us, and wet and cold even unto death. I found a knapsack cast on the shore, in which I had a steel and flint and powder-horn. Going further, I found a drowned goat; then I found a hat and my son William's coat, both which I put on. My wife found one of her petticoats which she put on. I found also two cheeses and some butter driven ashore. Thus the Lord sent us some clothes to put on, and food to sustain our new lives, which we had lately given unto us, and means also to make fire; for in a horn I had some gunpowder, which, to mine own, and since to other men's admiration, was dry.

"There we remained until the Monday following; when, about three of the clock in the afternoon, in a boat that came that way, we went off that desolate island, which I named, after my name, Thatcher's Woe, and the rock, Avery his Fall, to the end that their fall and loss, and mine own, might be had in perpetual remembrance."[1]

[1] Young's Chronicles, p. 485.

The worthy tailor's hope in this latter regard has been fully gratified. Thatcher's Island, at the head of Cape Ann, still perpetuates the remembrance of Thatcher's Woe, and Avery's Rock still puts us in mind of Avery his Fall.

CHAPTER IX.

FOR some fifteen years after the dissolution, in 1635, of the trading company of Laconia, and the partition of the Isles of Shoals between Gorges and Mason, they remained substantially free and independent. In that year, 1635, Mason died, and, for a long time afterwards, his heirs delayed to assert their title to the south half of the Shoals, or any part of the Province of New Hampshire. The northern half was, it is true, attached to Gorges' Province, but so loosely that the restraint of its courts was hardly felt. During this long period of independence, the Isles of Shoals made important advances in population, business and wealth. The inhabitants became sedentary; numbers of dwelling-houses were erected, and the titles to these bare rocks became of substantial value, worthy of careful record in the County books. The number of the resident population ran up to about 600 souls; "they had a meeting-house on Hog Island; a court-house on Haley's Island, and a seminary of such repute, that even gentlemen from some of the towns on the sea coast sent their sons here for literary instruction."[1]

The meeting-house is said to have been constructed of brick; the dwelling-houses of the more substantial residents were comfortable and of good size, the furniture as ample as then known in New England. An ordinary, or tavern, was kept on Smutty Nose, a bowling alley was on Hog Island, and ale houses abounded.[2] Flocks and herds, strange to relate, were not unknown upon the Islands. Philip Babb, in 1671, kept five head of cattle and seven sheep; William Seeley at the same time kept four sheep and several "shoates"; and other residents, no doubt, were proprietors of domestic animals. The soil of the islands was much deeper in those early days than it is at present. About the beginning of the present century, a great deal of the turf is said to have been consumed as fuel by the destitute islanders, and the soil has now become so scanty, that but for the extinction of the settlement, burials must, ere this, have been made in the sea.

The estates of the leading men at this early period were very large—among the largest in New England.

[1] 1 Williamson's Hist. of Maine, p. 277.

[2] York County Records, *passim.*

Philip Babb, according to the inventory recorded in the York County Records, left an estate, in 1671, valued at £200, and William Seeley's property was appraised in 1672 at £631 7s., sterling money.

For the first fifty years the population of the Isles of Shoals was chiefly located on the northern or Gorges portion, although Star Island was not wholly vacant. The earliest of the settlements had been made upon Hog Island, on account of a good spring of water there. A considerable village was built on the sheltered southerly slope of that Island, running back from Smith's Cove to the eastward, and straggling here and there over the rocks up the broken slope. The visitor of to-day may easily trace the general figure of the hamlet in the cellar and garden walls (some 70 or 80 in number), which, though now tumbled down and overgrown with vines and weeds, clearly mark the site of a once thriving village.

The Island, called Smutty Nose (now Haley's) possessed, in its smoother surface and arable fields, superior attractions over the rest of the group, as a place of residence. From the very first, accordingly, we find considerable numbers, and those among the chief of the population, selecting that Island as the site of their dwellings and fishing stages. Star Island remained for many years comparatively unoccupied.

The precise period, when the several Islands of the group acquired their present names, cannot now be fixed. As long as the population remained concentrated upon the large Island of the cluster, the name "Isle of Shoals" would be quite definite enough to designate that particular Island, though it was also used sometimes, in a larger sense, to denote the whole group. As soon, however, as the other Islands became inhabited, convenience would require the application to them of separate names. Until the dissolution of the Company of Laconia, the only name given to the Islands, whether general or specific, was that of the Isle or Isles of Shoals. The name of Hog Island we have traced back to 1635,[1] that of Smutty Nose to about 1650, and that of Star Island to 1651, though the latter names were, doubtless, conferred prior to those several dates.

Hog Island is said to have derived its name from the fancied resemblance of its elevated ridge to a hog's back. Smutty Nose was so nick-named from a long black projection or nose on its southeast side. Star Island derives its title from its star-shaped outline. Upon Cedar Island grew, perhaps, the "three or four short shrubby old cedars," spoken of by Captain Smith, which gave the Island its name, and the view of which

[1] Richard Mather's Journal. Young's Chronicles, p. 469.

by John Winthrop, as he sailed by in 1629, misled him into describing the Isles of Shoals as being "*woody.*"

The appellation of Isles of Shoals—spelt variously in early times, Shoulds or Sholes—was perhaps conferred on the group, on account of the reefs or shoals, which lurk about the Islands. The French maps translate the title, *Iles de battures*—or Isles of reefs.[2]

It is not our purpose to enter into minute details, as to the names, characters or genealogies of the early settlers upon our then busy islets. Such particulars could interest none but the devoted antiquary. Among the principal residents there, however, about the middle of the seventeenth century, when the Islands had attained a high prosperity, we may mention the three brothers from Wales, John, Richard and Robert Cutt. They seem to have settled upon Star Island, and although they all removed to the mainland about 1647, Richard and John carried on business at the Shoals

[1] Winthrop's Diary.

[2] It is proper to observe, however, that one of the most learned and exact antiquaries of New England, Charles W. Tuttle, Esq., of Boston, is of opinion that "the name of the group was obviously suggested by their plurality." On Captain Smith's map he says: "Eighteen distinct islands are laid down. A number that suggests the idea of a 'Shoal of Isles,' shoal being current in those days to signify a multitude, a throng or a crowd. Writers have chosen to write 'Isles of Shoals,' in place of 'Shoals of Isles,' thereby concealing to some extent the origin of the name."

until their death.[1] Richard Cutt seems, indeed, from his last will and testament, to have owned the whole of Star Island at the time of his death in 1676, and to have carried on an extensive trade there in partnership with his son-in-law, William Vaughan. John Cutt was, in 1679, created the first Royal President of the Province of New Hampshire. Robert Cutt was an Episcopalian and Royalist, like most of the founders of Maine and New Hampshire ; but his brothers, Richard and John, were strongly tinctured with Puritanism, and, perhaps on that account, preferred to carry on their extensive business at the Shoals on an island apart from the rest of the population. It was not probably until the death of Richard Cutt that Star Island was thrown open to general settlement, and from that time, as we shall hereafter see, it gradually attracted to itself the entire population of the group.

The three brothers, William, Richard and John Seeley were also among the more distinguished of the early settlers there. They came over from England before 1640, and established themselves on Smutty Nose Island, where for many years they occupied chief positions as magistrates, constables, deputies and merchants.[2]

[1] See their Last Wills. Brewster's Rambles, p. 29.

[2] York County Records.

Another group of brothers, William, Roger and John Kelly, make a considerable figure in the early records of the Shoals, as men of energy and substance. They also settled upon Smutty Nose. A fourth group of brothers, living on that Island at this time, were William, Benedict and Richard Oliver, who not only acquired there "dwelling-houses, houseings, staging and stage-room, flakes and flake-room and mooring places," in the language of the ancient deeds, but also purchased tracts of territory on the mainland.

The singular circumstance, that so many groups of brothers are found among our early emigrants is due to the fact that most of them were young unmarried men, and naturally sought the companionship of their brothers in emigrating to a new world.

The brothers, Michael and Richard Endel, (or Endle) emigrated to the Shoals about 1650, while very young men. They subsequently married young women of the Islands, accumulated property, and exercised considerable influence for many years.

Among the many other names to be met with in the ancient records of the Islands, are those of William Pepperell, father of Sir William Pepperell, William Wormwood, Gabriel Grubb, Walter Boaden, the brothers Peter and John Twisden, Herculus Hunkins, Philip Babb, Nick Hodge, the brothers Stephen and Richard Forde (alias Downs), Jack Crossom, Arthur Clapham, Fortunatus Home, and others equally queer. But the most attractive figure among all these early settlers is that of Mistress Rebecca Sherburne, wife of Henry Sherburne, who made her home for a time on the small Island of Malaga. Ambrose Gibbins and his wife, Rebecca's parents, had settled in New Hampshire as early as 1631. Ambrose, who had been for the previous ten years interested in New England matters, was sent out by Captain Mason as a steward or manager of the affairs of the Laconia Company, and resided in that capacity at Newitchawannock (now South Berwick) until about the time of the dissolution of that company; when, having procured from them a grant of Saunders' Point in Little Harbor, he removed his family there, and established a home on that beautiful locality.

His daughter, Rebecca, was a mere child at the time of her arrival in New Hampshire, probably the first white child ever resident within the limits of that Province. She was naturally a favorite in the settlement, and always spoken of in pleasant terms. For instance, George Vaughan writes to her father, in 1634: "My kind love to you and your spouse, and little Beck,"[1] and John Raymond, while riding in the

[1] 1 New Hamp. Prov. Pap., p. 95.

harbor of the Shoals, before sailing away to England, sends back to him a letter, remembering "my love to yourself, Mrs. Gibbins, little Becke, and the rest."[1]

The association of our little Becke with the Isles of Shoals, thus early begun, was destined to endure for many years. When she had reached about her seventeenth year she married Henry Sherburne. A few years after, her husband purchased, in 1647, of Antipas Maverick, a dwelling-house on Appledore Island; and there it is possible the young pair for a while resided. After a time, however, they removed to the little Island known as Malaga (then written *Malagoe*), and lived there probably at intervals, until 1660, when they sold out their property at the shoals to Nath'l. Freyer, and took up their future home on the mainland.[2] Little Becke seems, as is fitting, to have lived a prosperous and happy life, and her descendants are still numerous in the land.

The trade and commerce of the Isles of Shoals at this period was by no means insignificant. Not only were vast quantities of fish taken and cured by the fishermen of the Islands, but the harbor became the entrepot for the fish caught in other parts of the Gulf of Maine,[3] and were thence exported "to

[1] New Hampshire Pro. Pap., p. 76.
[2] 1 Id., p. 357.
[3] Lechford's "Plain Dealing," p. 116.

Lisbourne, Bilbo, Talloon, Rochel, and other cities of France, together with claw-boards and pipe-staves, which is there and at the Charibs a prime commodity,"[1] bringing rich return cargoes of wine, sugar, tobacco, etc., which were distributed from the warehouses of the traders at the Shoals and Strawberry Bank among the various settlements from Martha's Vineyard to Acadia. In 1636, for instance, Thomas Mayhew visited the Shoals for the purpose of purchasing so large a quantity as eighty hogsheads of provisions at one time, and expended a hundred pounds sterling in imported "ruggs and coates."[2]

It was from these busy Islets that voyagers to the old world often embarked, and prisoners of state, ordered to be transported to England, were sent out to the Isles of Shoals to take passage in vessels bound from thence. The famous Thomas Morton, of Merry Mount, one of the first victims of the intolerance of the Pilgrim Fathers, was, in 1628, banished from New England in a vessel, which sailed from these Islands in June of that year.[3] As Morton, after many tribulations, finally settled down at the Piscataqua, and passed there the remainder of his life, we have felt

[1] Josselyn's Voyages to New England, p. 161.

[2] Mass. Hist. Col., 4th Series, Vol. VII., p. 31.

[3] Morton's New England Memorial, p. 141.

a curiosity to discover the grievous offences, which justified so severe a punishment as banishment, and the confiscation or destruction of his estate. One of his chief sins proven seems to have been a mirthful and sportive temper, and the evidence of it was that he and his merry men were guilty of dancing around a Maypole—*a calfe of Horeb*, groaned the Puritans—and of composing a profane, licentious song, which was sung, says Morton himself, "with a Corus, every man bearing his part; which they performed in a daunce, hand-in-hand about the Maypole, whiles one of the Company sung, and filled out the good liquor, like Gannemede and Jupiter."

The song itself, if any of our readers may desire to glance at so wicked a composition, ran thus: —

THE SONGE.

Drinke, and be merry, merry, merry boyes,
Let all your delight be in Hymen's joyes,
Io to Hymen, now the day is come,
About the merry Maypole take a roome.
　　Make greene garlons, bring bottles out,
　　And fill sweet Nectar freely about;
　　Uncover thy head and feare no harm,
　　For here's good liquor to keep it warme.

Then drinke and be merry, etc.
　　Nectar is a thing assigned
　　By the Deitie's owne mind
　　To cure the hart oppressed with griefe,
　　And of good liquors is the chiefe.

Then drinke, etc.
Give to the mellancolly man
A cup or two of 't now and then;
This physick will soone revive his bloud,
And make him of a merrier moode.

Then drinke, etc.
Give to the Nymphe that's free from scorne
No Irish stuff, nor Scotch o'erworne;
Lasses in beaver coats come away,
Yee shall be welcome to us night and day.
Then drinke and be merry boys, etc.[1]

The dancing about a Maypole, the other chief article in Morton's indictment, was a hearty old English pastime, by no means uncommon with the first planters. Phinehas Pratt, who visited the Isles of Shoals as early as 1622, the year before the arrival of Capt. Levett, was guilty, on his own confession, of the same sin. Pratt, in company with nine others, arrived at Damariscove Island in May, 1622, in the ship "Sparrow." He informs us, in his curious and quaint Narrative, that they went ashore, "set up a Maypole and were very merry."

Phinehas, with some others of the merry makers, then left the ship and sailed along the coast in a boat towards Mass. Bay. "We first arrived," he writes, "att Smithe's Islands, first soe called by Capt. Smith,

[1] Morton's New English Canaan, p. 91.

att the time of his discovery of New England, afterwards called 'Ilands of Sholes.'"

Having then proceeded to Plymouth and Wessaguscus, the next spring, March, 1623, he returned to the Isles of Shoals, and rejoined his ship, the Sparrow, in that harbor.

"At this time," says Phinehas, in his manuscript, now partly illegible, "ships began to fish at ye Islands of Sholes, and I, having recovered a little of my health, went to my company, nearabout this time . . . . the first plantation att Pascataqua the . . . . thereof was Mr. David Tomson, at the time of my arrival att Pascataqua."[1]

Not only did voyagers and banished men and fishermen seek vessels at the Shoals, but the islands seem to have become a chief emporium of foreign news.

For instance, Gorges writes to Winthrop, in 1640, from Gorgeanna (now York): "I cannot send you news from England, because the contrariety of winds

[1] "At the time of his (Captain Levett) being at Pascataway," (1623,) continues Phinehas Pratt, "a Sacham or Sagamor gave two of his men, one to Capt. Levett, and another to Mr. Tomson; but one that was there said, "How can you trust those salvages? Call the name of one 'Watt Tyler' and ye other 'Jack Straw,' (Cade) after the names of the two greatest Rebills yt ever were in England." — Phinehas Pratt's Narrative.

hath hindred it from coming from the Isles of Shoals;"[1] and the great tidings of the breaking out of the English rebellion, as well as the news of the execution of King Charles in 1649, did not reach New England until it was brought out by a Shoals' vessel."[2]

Indeed, if it were consonant to the plan of this sketch to accumulate still further instances and details of the active prosperity of the Isles of Shoals, during the middle of the seventeenth century, abundant evidences might be gathered out of the Mass. Colonial Records, the New Hampshire Provincial Papers, and the Records of York County and of Kittery, to which we must content ourselves at present, with simply making a reference.

[1] 7 Mass. Hist. Col., 4th Series, p. 334.
[2] 2 Winthrop, pp. 60, 413. Savage's Notes.

CHAPTER X.

THE Isles of Shoals remained at the height of their prosperity for about twenty years after the dissolution of the Company of Laconia, to which they had belonged; during which period they enjoyed almost unrestrained civil and religious liberty. At last, about 1652, they fell under the dominion of Massachusetts Bay.

The dissensions between the King and Commons of England, which, as we have seen, began partly in the grievances of the poor fishermen of the Gulf of Maine, as early as 1622, had deepened in importance and bitterness, until, in 1640, the nation was on the eve of that momentous struggle which was, for the next decade, to plunge the kingdom in blood and anarchy. The Massachusetts colony, who deeply sympathized with the Roundheads throughout the rebellion, and were confident of the latter's support in the usurpation they meditated, considered the occasion auspicious to seize upon the Provinces of New Hampshire and Maine, under the pretext that a true construction of their charter extended their northern limits as far as Clapboard Island, in Casco Bay.

Accordingly, in 1640, following the example of Joshua, the son of Nun, Gov. Winthrop sent into those parts the famous Hugh Peters, to "view the land," and sound the inclinations of the people. The messenger returned and reported to the Governor, that the people of the Easterly provinces were, in his own words, "ripe for our Government, as will appear by the note I have sent you. They grone for Government and Gospell all over that side of the country. Alas, poore bleeding soules!"[1] Some of the people of the Piscataqua were then procured to sign a petition for admission, and accordingly, in 1641, that section of the country was taken under the protecting wing of the Mass. Bay,[2] and so remained for nearly forty years afterwards. The Province of Maine, however, stood out against the arguments and allurements of Governor Winthrop for ten years longer; but when at last King Charles, in 1649, perished on the scaffold, and the cause of

[1] 6 Mass. Hist. Col., 4th Series, p. 108.

[2] 1 New Hamp. Prov. Pap., 158.

the Roundheads was triumphant, the Puritans of Massachusetts had no longer any punishment to dread for their deed of violence, and as soon, therefore, as the necessary arrangements could be perfected, they took possession of the Province of Maine, which, by "hook and crook," they managed to hold for nearly two centuries after.

The Isles of Shoals, during the progress of this struggle between Maine and Massachusetts, ranged themselves stoutly on the side of their royalist and Episcopalian friends on the mainland. When the New Hampshire towns submitted to the Bay rulers in 1641, the Shoals openly revolted against the Puritan Roundheads, and declared their independence. Their minister, Richard Gibson, of the Church of England, who was settled at the Shoals in 1641 and 1642, spared no pains nor zeal to confirm his people in their resolution. Being in Boston in the summer of the latter year, on his return to England, he was seized by the authorities there, and indicted for "exercising the ministerial function at the Shoals according to the discipline of the Church of England, opposing the Mass. title to those parts, and provoking the people to revolt"; but as it turned out that Master Gibson was then "upon the wing of removal" from the country, it was thought better to suspend further proceedings against him.[1]

When, however, the province of Maine, in 1652, was compelled to bow before the Mass. Bay, the Isles of Shoals could no longer maintain the attitude of open resistance. The whole group were then brought into nominal obedience to the Bay, and so remained for nearly thirty years thereafter. A sound Puritan minister, the Rev. John Brock, was sent over to them. Three judges or commissioners to "end small causes" were appointod among them by the Puritans;[2] "constables and a Sargeant Major" were empowered, "to preserve order among them and to train their militia"; and so heavy a tax was imposed on them and Kittery, to which the northerly half was then annexed, as to amount to half the sum assessed upon the entire county of Yorkshire.[3]

The following year, 1653, some twenty of the principal inhabitants petitioned the Mass. Gen. Court that the Islands might be erected into a separate township, and for certain other privileges therein specified. As this petition set forth clearly the considerable population of the Shoals at this period, as well as several other

[1] 2 Winthrop's Hist., p. 66.
[2] Mass. Rec., Vol. IV., Part i., p. 133.
[3] Mass. Rec., Vol. IV., Part i., p. 283.

matters of interest, we hope to be pardoned for quoting it, *in extenso.* It runs as follows: —

To the much honored Court held at Boston, ye 18th of ye 3d,53.
The humble petition of the Inhabitants in the Isles of Shoules
Sheweth

That whereas wee the said Inhabitants liveing so remote from the neighbuor-townes upon the Maine and having thereby allready sustained much vexinge through want of a power deputed amongst our selves to helpe, whom it may concerne to their due debts, and findinge alsoe by unsutable wind and weather, that wee cannot (upon occasion) visite the Court that we might enjoy the benefitt of the Law, to recover our owne, in way righteousnes. Wee therefore upon such like reasons doe thinke it our dutie to make petition to this much honored general Court that you mought be pleased to take our condition into your serious and sage consideration & to grant us the privilege of a Towneshipp, as farre as your wisdomes shall think us capable, as that we may have amongst us a Clarke of the Writts & some others authorized to have the hearing & issuing of such causes as may fall out under the summe of Ten pounds, we finding as wee under your favor, more neede of such a prevelege than our neighbor-townes, forasmuch as some of our transient ones as it may fall out, they cannot tarrie untill their causes may be issued elsewhere.

Alsoe, may it please the honored Court to take notice that our situation is such, as many times wee necessarilie shall not be able to joyne with our neighbors in militarie affaires through unseasonable weather, without great hazard or damage to ourselves. Our request is therefore that, you would be pleased to make us a distinct company in that respect, wee being upwards of a hundred men at this time, & that our loving friends John Arthur Lieut: & William Sealy Ensigne so chosen amongst us, to beginne that service, they mought be instated into such places, for the benefit of the rest, according to your order.

Thus wee nothing doubting, but yee will be pleased to pass by any of these our unsuitable expressions, & grant us whatsoever your discretion shall see mostly conduceing to our best good. Wee for your fatherlie ceare allready enjoyed, & yet expected doe account our selves in bounden dutie to be ready, to doe you any service to our abilitie, & to make supplications yet in your behalfe, for the further influences of the holie ghost upon your hearts, in these approaching & all after agitations, for his own glory, with his churches wellfare. We now humblie take our leave, & subscribe in the name & with general consent.

Hercules Hunkins	John Arthur
Rice Cadogan	Edward Smale
Samuel Jewell	Benjamin Bickford
Rice Joanes	Phillip Babb
William Sealy	Peter Gee
William Vren	Walther Mathews
Peter Twisden	Richard Sealy
John Bickford	Humphrey Horewell
John Bretnell	Mathew Giles
John Fabins	George Sealy

This document was copied by Charles W. Tuttle, Esq., from the original on file in the office of the Secretary of State in Boston. Every signer, says Mr. Tuttle, "wrote his name in a good fair hand. Upon its reception, the Court ordered that the inhabitants of the 'Isles of Shoals' have liberty to determine all civil actions, where either or both parties are inhabitants, to the value of ten pounds. A 'Clark of the Writts' was authorized to be appointed; but the modest request to be made a township was ignored."

In 1659, the inhabitants of all the islands again petitioned the Massachusetts General Court to be created a separate township.[1] This petition was at first denied, on the ground that "the Court doe not judge the persons petitioning to be in a capacity at present to make a township."[2] The reason of the Gen. Court's rejection of this petition was, probably, that at this time, there were few or no persons residing there, who were members of the established Puritan Church in good standing; and at that time, indeed, such a church had not been gathered in the orthodox way. Two years later, however, the petition was renewed with better success. In 1661, it was ordered, that the whole group "shall be reputed and hereby allowed to be a township called Apledoore,[3] and shall have

[1] 4 Mass. Rec., Part i., p. 375.

[2] Id., p. 136.

[3] The name *Appledore* was derived, according to the opinion of Charles W. Tuttle, Esq., from that of an ancient hamlet, in the parish of *Northam,* on the coast of Barnstaple Bay, in North Devonshire. The appellation of *Northam* was originally conferred upon the town on the Piscataqua, now called Dover.

It was from Devonshire and Cornwall that the first planters of New Hampshire and Maine chiefly emigrated, and they naturally bestowed upon their new homes the familiar names of their beloved towns and hamlets in the old world.

The village of Appledore was once famous for its great castle, called *Kinwith,* in ancient days; at the siege of which, saith old Camden, "in the yeare of Christ, 879, Hubba, the

equall power to regulate their towne affaires, as other townes of this jurisdiction have."[1]

It will be observed that the Islands were by this act created a township, only for the "regulating their towne affairs." The ancient division was maintained in full force for County and Provincial purposes, and must have subjected the inhabitants to a considerable inconvenience, which was not obviated until 1672. In that year, in compliance with the petition of the islanders for redress of this grievance, it was ordered that the whole group "be adjoined unto the same county, unto which Star Island belongs,"[2] in

Dane, who, with many slaughters and overthrows, had harried the English nation, was (with many other Danes) slaine. And then it was that the Englishmen won the Danes' banner, called *Reafan* . . . The Danes bare in this Ensign a Raven wrought (by report) in needle worke by the daughters of Lothbrooke, that is *Leatherbreech*, the Dane, with such an opinion of good luck, as they thought it could never be wonne." — *Camden's Britannia*, p. 208.

This prophetic raven, adds another writer, drooped its wings before defeat, and clapped them triumphantly before a victory.

The fortunes of the ancient Appledore has not been unlike that of her younger namesake. By the latest gazeteer, it appears that trade and the fisheries have now deserted the venerable hamlet, but "as there is an extensive beach and good accommodation for strangers, Appledore is fast growing into notice as a bathing and watering place."

1 New Hamp. Prov. Pap., p. 240.

2 4 Mass. Rec., Part ii., p. 520.

other words, to the County of Dover and Portsmouth, and the Province of New Hampshire.

This union was brief; in the year 1679, the connection between New Hampshire and Mass. Bay, which had now lasted for nearly forty years, was finally broken by the erection of New Hampshire into a Royal Province, under the presidency of a former resident and merchant of the Shoals, Mr. John Cutt.

In this commission, the Isles of Shoals, by some oversight, were not mentioned; but in that issued in 1682 to Cranfield, it was held, by construction, that the south half was included, though not expressly named, and a warrant was issued to bring the inhabitants into obedience.[1] In subsequent royal commissions, the southerly half of the Islands was embraced by name.

The original division of the group was now restored, the township of "Apledoore" was dissolved; the north half returned to Maine, and the southerly half was laid off once more to New Hampshire, a partition which has never since been disturbed.[2]

The dividing line, as subsequently confirmed by the Commissioners of the two Provinces, in 1737, ran 'through the middle of the harbor between the islands,

[1] 1 N. H. Prov. Pap., p. 132.

[2] Belknap's Hist. of New Hamp., p. 151.

to the sea, on the southerly side."[1] This boundary line was reaffirmed, in 1820, by convention between New Hampshire and Maine.

[1] 2 Belknap's Hist. of New Hamp., p. 114.

CHAPTER XI.

ABOUT this period, a remarkable change took place in the distribution of the population among the Islands. From the earliest settlements down to the erection of New Hampshire into a Royal Province, the inhabitants had chiefly dwelt on the northerly half of the group, Hog Island and Smutty Nose. About this time, however, a large part of the people, for some unexplained cause, removed over to Star Island on the New Hampshire side. No less than forty families, according to tradition, crossed over from Hog Island at one time. This reason of this exodus, usually assigned, is that Star Island was thought more secure against assaults from the Indians. It is difficult to perceive the superiority of Star Island in this respect, and the true cause of the change must now be left to conjecture.

If we are correct in the inference previously mentioned, that Richard Cutt continued the exclusive proprietor of Star Island up to the time of his death, the removal may have followed upon the throwing open that Island to general settlement after his decease, and may have been prompted by the superior convenience of Star Island for the prosecution of the fisheries.

At all events, the northerly half of the group began at this time to be greatly depopulated. By 1688, the population and wealth of the northerly Islands had become so much reduced, that in a general rate or assessment of £41.14s, upon the Province of Maine, these Islands were charged with but £1.10s.[1] Twenty or thirty years later, we are informed by a doleful petition from Kittery for the remission of taxes, that there were seldom at "the Isle Shoals (the north half thereof) more than ten or fifteen persons rateable, and they were all poor; had about three or four small boats for fishing, and they never paid half the rates and taxes that was added to the town of Kittery, upon the account of their being annexed to it; and besides that, as soon as they joined to Kittery several poor families came from thence to the town for support, which cost the town more money than all the rates and taxes that ever the Isle Shoals paid to Kittery, exclusive of the charges since their being so annexed.

[1] Records of York County.

For several years past, the Isle Shoals has paid no taxes at all, though the town was taxed for them every year."[1]

This petition of Kittery to be relieved from taxation sets the singular poverty of that town, of which the north half of the Shoals was a part, in such a thoroughly convincing, if not ludicrous light, that perhaps our readers may be amused with an epitome of it.

"The township of Kittery," say the petitioners, "is a long strip of land, a great part unprofitable; about one quarter part of the lands in said town are not capable of any improvement in husbandry. Such mossy, rocky ground and boggy swamps, as bear nothing to support any useful creatures, is not profitable for anything. Poor fishermen, and sailors, and some laborers purchased small house lotts here and there amongst the rocks, built little cottages to live in, on which lotts some may raise a bushell of Potatoes and a hundred cabbages, and many cannot raise as much; and those cottages make a great part of the number of houses (so called) throughout the town of Kittery. In the whole town are about 284 families, and one quarter of them cannot raise one bushel of corn or

[1] See this Petition in 4th Maine Hist. Col., p. 204.

any sort of grain, in a year, nor are they able to raise a supply of any sort of provisions, but depend upon others for their supply. Not one in ten, through the whole town, does raise a full sufficiency for their own familys to live on the year about. The town in general depend upon buying, but have nothing to purchase withall. The fishery is dwindled into nothing. Not one fishing vessel in the town improved; the fishermen driven to other business and lost, leaving their poor and helpless widows and familys to the town for support. In a great many of these houses is nothing but a continual cry of hunger, poverty and want.

"There is not any one commodity of the produce of the town of Kittery, sufficient to supply the whole town with what is necessary for their own use. The inhabitants don't make, nor are they able to make, one half of their own clothing, neither is all the cattle annually raised in the town sufficient to supply the town with meat.

"The town of Kittery produces no lumber nor any other commodity for any market, not so much as one half part of what is used in the town.

"There is but two merchants in the town and their trading cannot be any thing of the produce of the town; but the goods they bring to trade upon, they trust out to the poor, many of whom never pay.

"There has been very little building of ships in Kittery, for many years past. Tradesmen have little or nothing to do, farmers have nothing to spare, and others have nothing to live upon.

"There is not three rich men in the town, most all are very poor. Many are wretched and miserable. Kittery has not wood and timber enough for their own use. Kittery is the least quantity of land of any town in the county.

"No person liveing can show that Kittery does produce any one commodity to trade upon, of any sort; but poor widows and orphans they have in plenty, more than any other town in the country. The Province bills never depreciated in their value so much, as Kittery has depreciated in its value. It has nothing to shew but integrity and honesty for its support, and poverty for its defence.

"We subscribe ourselves, in behalf of the poor town of Kittery; Your Humble Servants,

Jos. Hammond and others."

It is to be hoped that the rueful town of Kittery, to which the north half of the Isles of Shoals was then and has ever since been attached, experienced some measure of relief from this lamentable petition. It would be difficult to present the justice of their supplication in a stronger or more moving light.

From the beginning of the eighteenth century, we thus perceive, the northerly, or Gorges half of the Isles of Shoals had become almost deserted. It was upon Star Island, on the New Hampshire side, that from the time of the royal charter of that Province, in 1679, the population and business of the group was concentrated, and for a century after that period, continued to flourish there.

In 1715, by Act of the New Hampshire Provincial Assembly, Star Island was created a town, by the name of Gosport[1] (sometimes written Gosper), and five years later, its prosperous condition is shown from the report of a Committee, imposing a rate of £20 in every £1000 raised in the Province,[2] a proportion which, as appears from the records, was nearly maintained for many years after. Even as late as 1767 the number of residents at Gosport was 284, among whom were four slaves.[3]

Upon the outbreak of the war with the French and their Indian allies in 1745, which resulted in the renowned capture of Louisburg by Sir William Pepperell, son of the William Pepperell, who had been an early resident of the Shoals, it was deemed prudent that

[1] 3 New Hamp. Prov. Pap., p. 620.

[2] 3 N. H. Prov. Pap., p. 783.

[3] 1 Farmer and Moore, N. H. Hist. Col., p. 166.

some precautions should be taken at these exposed Islets, against the assaults of the French cruisers. Accordingly, a small fort was erected on an eminence near the western point of Star Island, and mounted with nine four-pounders. The ruins of this fortification are said to have been still visible in 1800. The fort was dismantled on the outbreak of the Revolutionary war, and the guns sent to Newburyport.[1] At the time of the erection of this fort, the Province of New Hampshire voted, in answer to the Petition of "ye inhabitants of Gosport, they be allow'd fifteen pounds to purchase ammunition, the money to be paid to ye selectmen of said Gosport for ye use of sd town out of ye publick Treasury."[2]

The Islands, if attacked, seem to have defended themselves throughout that French and Indian war with success, but on the outbreak of the war of the Revolution, "as it was found that these Islands afforded sustenance and recruits to the enemy, early in the war, the inhabitants were ordered to quit the Islands. In obedience to government, the greater part of the people dispersed into the seaport towns along the coast, and most of them never after returned; about twenty

[1] 7 Mass. Hist. Coll., 1st Ser., p. 246.

[2] 5 N. H. Prov. Pap., p. 493.

families removed to Old York, where their descendants now live."

The only evidence we have discovered, on the subject of the patriotism of the Shoalers during our struggle for independence, is in the Gosport Records; where is to be found the following entry:

"11 Mch., 1775, for *histing the flag*, to Henry Andres 20s."

Which flag may be left to the fancy of the reader.[1]

So general was, at this time, the dispersion of the people, that in 1775 only forty-four persons were remaining on the islands.[2]

At the close of the Revolutionary war, a few of the former inhabitants straggled back to their dilapidated cabins on Gosport; but their ancient prosperity has never since revived. In 1790, Belknap informs us, the population had recovered to 93, and in 1800, as appears from the Gosport town records, their number was 112, "including solitaries," most of them,

[1] This fact is one of those for which the author is indebted to Mr. D. P. Corey, of Malden. While these pages were going through the press, Mr. Corey generously placed at our disposal his large and most valuable collection of materials on the subject. Had these papers fallen into our hands earlier, much of our laborious research would have been dispensed with. The manuscripts of Mr. Corey display remarkable antiquarian zeal and learning.

[2] 3 Belknap, p. 227.

continues the record, "in a state of great poverty and wretchedness, such as to force the tear of commiseration, and to draw from the humane every effort to afford relief."

In 1819, the number of residents on the Islands had become reduced to 86, and in 1824 to 69; since which time, the population has continued to dwindle away, year by year, until hardly one individual remains of the ancient race. The town of Gosport, though perhaps a formal town organization may be still kept up, has become practically extinct, and Star Island, swept clean of its weather-beaten cabins and unsavory fish houses, has been dedicated to the entertainment of the valetudinarian and the summer idler.

CHAPTER XII.

THE Islands, whose decay we have traced, enjoyed one advantage over the mainland, which, no doubt, contributed materially to their early prosperity — we mean their general exemption from Indian depredations. Capt. Christopher Levett fails not to perceive this advantage, in his visit of 1623. "Upon these Islands," says he, "are no savages at all." The brave islanders, however, did not fail to come to the aid of their more exposed brethren on the mainland, in the emergencies of our numerous Indian wars. The marvellous escape of John Abbott, of the Shoals, from captivity at the hands of the eastern tribes, in 1676, as recorded by Hubbard, in his "History of the Indian Wars in New England," may perhaps interest our readers.

John Abbott, who has been described as one of the "meteoric class of heroes," was probably in the employment of Nathaniel Freyer, at his fishing establishment on Malaga Island, which, as we have seen, had been purchased by him in 1660, from Henry Sherburne and his wife, *little Becky.* In company with young James Freyer, Abbott had sailed to Richman's Island, in 1676, in a ketch belonging to Freyer, and had there been surprised by a considerable band of savages, under the command of a famous Sagamore, named Mugg. Freyer was mortally wounded, the remainder of the company taken prisoners, and all except John Abbott carried away captives towards Canada. The ketch was removed eastward to Shipscot River, with Abbott on board, and moored there all the next winter.

"In which time," continues Hubbard, "the Indians, having spent all their ammunition, etc., counted it high time to be looking out for more; to which end they caused the said Abbott to fit up the vessel (being a pinnace of about thirty Tun) as well as he could, with such assistance as they could afford him; and ten of them shipped themselves in the same, intending for Penobscott, and thence to pass on to Canada, in their canoes, to buy powder of the French there. But as Providence ordered it, after these Marriners were launched into the Deep, a small storm with contrary winds began to arise; of which the English skipper found wayes in his steering to make the danger seem more than really it was, insomuch that they resolved to put in at Cape bona-waggon, three leagues to the eastward of Shipscot; where eight of them went ashore, leaving two Indians aboard with the English skipper. After he had got so well rid of them, he contrived how to get shut of the others also. Therefore he persuaded them that the vessel would not ride well in that place, so as he prevailed with them to let him go to another harbor called Damaris Cove, two or three leagues more eastward. In the way, as he sayled, he so ordered his steering, that sometimes the waves were ready to overtake the vessel, which put his two Indians into a fright, so as they made all the haste they could to get ashore, as soon as ever they came in the harbor urging him to go along with them; but he pretended a necessary excuse to stay behind to look after the vessel, but with intent, as soon as ever he could see them ashore, to hoyse sayl for some English harbor, having nobody aboard with him but a small English child about three years old. It seems the Indians had a child or two of their own dead in the vessel, who dying after they began their voyage, they were forwarder to go ashore with them for buryal. The said Abbott, now perceiving he had obtained his purpose (for he oft resolved on this project before), first tallowing the mast with a piece of fat pork, left by the

Indians, as high as he could reach, that he with his own hands might the more easily hoyse the sayl, so choosing rather to cast himself upon the Providence of God in the waters, than to trust himself any longer with perfidious salvages on the dry land; he came safe to the Isle of Shoals, before the evening of the next day, February the nineteenth."[1]

A few years after this time, the Isles of Shoals narrowly escaped utter destruction at the hands of the French and Indians, during the distressing and sanguinary conflict, commonly known as "King William's war."

In that conflict, the whole coast of Maine and New Hampshire was devastated, and all the settlements in the former province utterly destroyed, except the four towns of Wells, Kittery, York and the Isles of Shoals. To capture and annihilate these remaining settlements, and thus close the war, the French and Indians, in 1691, resolved upon the most desperate efforts, with all the combined forces by land and sea, they could muster. Their design was, however, for the present, thwarted by an accidental conflict with the New England forces at Pejepscot falls. The next year, 1692, their attempt was renewed with a large

[1] 2 Hubbard's Ind. Wars, p. 210.

force. York was burned, and nearly all its inhabitants killed or taken prisoners; but the heroic resistance of the few remaining soldiers, in their block-house, at last compelled the retreat of the assailants. The baffled enemy then turned their assault upon the next remaining town, Wells. A force of 500 French and Indians, under their French officers, Burneffe and Labrocree, fell upon the garrison at Wells, defended by but fifteen soldiers, under command of the heroic Capt. Converse, reinforced, just before the assault, by two sloops, having on board fourteen men. The conflict, which now ensued, was one of the most desperate and bloody that had ever occurred in New England. The story of it, as related by Cotton Mather in his "Magnalia," is one of the most thrilling in our early annals; but it is not within our limits to do more than refer to its result. After a desperate fight of forty-eight hours, "prosecuted by a host against a handfull," the allies were beaten off with severe loss, and the projected expedition against the Isles of Shoals was again abandoned. Later in the same year, the attempt was renewed by a still heavier force, assisted by two French frigates. This last expedition was concerted at Quebec, between Count Frontenac, Governor of Canada, and the Indian Sagamore Madockawando, and would, probably, have prevailed, but for the brave patriotism of Mr. John Nelson. This gentleman, being at that time a prisoner in Quebec, obtained from Madockawando the secret of the projected enterprise, and at once, to the great hazard of his life, bribed two Frenchmen to carry intelligence of it to Boston.[1] The messengers were captured on their return, and shot to death as spies, and the patriotic Nelson himself was transported to France, and imprisoned five years in solitary confinement in the Bastille. But his warning gave New England time to prepare for the meditated blow, and thus proved the salvation of the Isles of Shoals, and the few other settlements still clinging to the coasts of Maine.

At the brave defence of Wells by Captain Converse, which we have spoken of, one John Diamond was taken prisoner by the Indians, and dragged away by his hair into the thickets. After their humiliating defeat, in their "nefandous rage," the savages put their captive to the most dreadful tortures. "They stripped him," writes Cotton Mather, "they scalped him alive; they slit him with knives between his fingers and toes; they made cruel gashes in the most fleshy parts of his body, and stuck the gashes with firebrands, which were afterwards found sticking in the wounds."[2]

[1] 1 Hutchinson, p. 338.

[2] 2 Mather's Mag., p. 535; 1 Williamson's Maine, p. 634.

Alas! This poor John Diamond was, probably, the son of Andrew Diamond (or Dymont), for many years a taverner and magistrate upon the Isles of Shoals, and himself, perhaps, sometimes a resident there.

In 1724, during the three years' or Lovewell's war, the savages made up a flotilla of fifty canoes, and strange to relate, carried on for a time a successful naval war along our coast. In a few weeks, they were in possession, by capture, of twenty-two vessels, several of good size, and one armed with swivels. They made an assault upon the Shoals, and succeeded in cutting out and carrying away two shallops, which they added to their fleet. The Indian squadron was pursued speedily by two vessels, with about forty men from New Hampshire, and followed into Penobscot, where a naval battle occurred, and victory pronounced for the savages. Shortly after, the Indians dispersed, and although other expeditions were fitted out against them, not a particle of intelligence concerning them could be afterward obtained.[1]

There is a tradition, that during King Philip's war, the savages invaded the Islands and carried away many female captives. One Betty Moody secreted

[1] Penhallow's Indian Wars, p. 103; 2 Hutchinson, p. 278; 2 Williamson, p. 128.

herself during the alarm in a remarkable chasm or cave, on the S.E. point of Star Island, which still bears her name. Others say she was drowned there.[1]

But although generally exempt from Indian atrocities, a pleasing manifestation of sympathy on the part of the residents of the Shoals with the sufferings of the mainland during the Indian wars, is recorded in our chronicles. In 1677, a contribution was raised throughout New England for the ransom of several inhabitants of Hatfield, in Massachusetts, who had been carried captive into Canada by the Indians. The benevolence of the Shoals, on this occasion, towards the distressed people of that remote town in Western Massachusetts, was very remarkable. The Isles of Shoals contributed to the fund a sum exceeding considerably the amount raised in Salem, while Kittery, whose miserable poverty is so movingly set forth in the petition we have quoted, surpassed in their benevolence the thriving town of Lynn.[2]

[1] 7 Mass. Hist. Coll., p. 244; 1 Williamson's Maine, p. 276.

[2] Drake's Boston, p. 430.

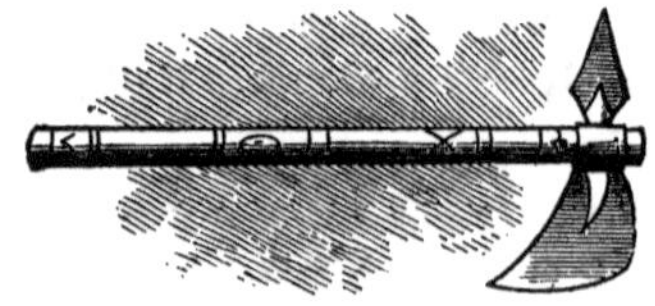

CHAPTER XIII.

THE population of the Isles of Shoals, whose political and social connection with New Hampshire and Maine, we have briefly, though, we fear, tediously traced, was not of a kind, after all, to be very deeply moved by questions of government, or much concerned with statutes or courts. While they remained annexed to Gorges' Province, the complaints of the Maine courts were frequent, of the difficulty, on account of their remoteness, of settling and maintaining order there.[1] And a considerable proportion of the criminal complaints against them were for resisting, assaulting and reviling the officers of the law, and treating with contempt the awe-inspiring badge of his office.[2] For instance, we

[1] York County Records.

[2] This badge, "that no man shall pleade ignorance when a constable shall call assistance," was required by statute to be "a staff, black and about five foote or five and a half foote long, tipped at ye upper end, about five or six inches, with brasse." Some years later (1735) these portentous staves were tipped at the Shoals with pewter.

read in the York County Records, how that Samuel Matthews and Abraham Kelley, of the Shoals, were indicted for abusing and reviling the constable there; Nicholas Hodges was presented for a similar offense; Robert Mace, "for abusing the constable by very opprobrious Languidg"; Richard Oliver, for resisting and treating contumeliously, the magistrate's mittimus; Stephen Forde, "for abusing the constable, and calling him rogue and rascall"; William Curtis, for assaulting his majesty's officer; Gabriel Grubb, for saying "he could find it in his heart to kill the constable," and Bartholomew Mitchell, Rebora Downs, and Bartholomew Burrington were charged with assailing the Shoals' constable "by words and blows, and threatening to break his neck on the rocks, and pulling off his neck cloth."[1]

The same spirit of insubordination remained among them, after the erection of New Hampshire, in 1679, into a Royal Province. In 1682, they are represented by the Council of New Hampshire to King Charles II., as "not being at present under any government at all";[2] and after the annexation of the south half to New Hampshire, abundant evidence exists of their utter indifference to the laws and courts of the

[1] York County Court Records.

[2] 1 Belknap, p. 151.

mainland. The north half was never represented in the Mass. Genl. Court but once,[1] and the south half very rarely, if ever, consented to send deputies to the New Hampshire Provincial Assembly, and paid little or no tribute to the Province rates.

In 1701, Mr. James Blagdon, one of the principal inhabitants of the Isles of Shoals, is ordered by the Council and General Assembly of the Province of New Hampshire, "to settle the inhabitants, where he lives, under this government, and to call them together to appoint a Representative for said place to sit in Genl. Assembly and to observe such further orders and directions as he shall receive from the Honble. the Lt. Govern. concerning the same."[2] As the Shoalites paid no manner of heed to this order, Star Island was again, in 1711, served with a warrant to send up a representative to the House;[3] and again in 1716,[4] but they paid no attention to either summons. The government, as a next resource, thought fit, in 1716, to annex Star Island to New Castle, for election and assessment purposes,[5] but the islanders neither attended the elections nor paid the rates.[6] At length their arrearages ran up, in 1761, to the sum of £512,

[1] 2 Williamson's Maine, p. 13.
[2] 3 N. H. Prov. Pap., p. 124.
[3] Id., p. 465.
[4] 4 Id., p. 617.
[5] 3 Id., p. 648.
[6] 4 Id., p. 623.

8s 1d, new tenor; and the Selectmen of Gosport procured a vote of the Provincial Assembly, that the whole debt should be abated.[1] Nor does it appear that the Provincial Government ever made any profit out of their recusant citizens of the Shoals, beyond, perhaps, a few pounds in the way of paying Province debts to the people of Gosport itself. For instance, in 1724, it seems that one Robert Saunders, of Star Island, had brought into Portsmouth intelligence of a "pirate ship hovering about the coast." The Gen. Assembly allowed him for this service the sum of 40 shillings, but very shrewdly added, "to be paid by the constable of Gosport, as he is behind hand in the payment of his Province rates for ye year 1723."[2] It is not probable that Robert ever realized any reward for what some of his neighbors regarded as his officiousness in reporting the pirate ship to the New Hampshire authorities. There is strong ground of suspicion, indeed, that the islanders were generally indulgent, and sometimes friendly and serviceable in their intercourse with the numerous pirate ships which visited their harbor.

After the organization of the present State Government of New Hampshire, at the close of the Revolu-

[1] 6 New Hamp. Prov. Pap., p. 795.

[2] 4 N. Hamp. Prov. Pap., p. 142.

tion, the Shoals had fallen, as we have seen, into such decay, as for many years to escape the notice of the officials; until, in a season of high political controversy, in the year 1851, a Democratic Legislature, regarding the handful of fishermen at Gosport as natural upholders of "free trade and sailor's rights," admitted their Representative to the House, since which they have annually elected one of their number to serve in the General Court.

This indifference, or rather dislike towards all established authority, to which we have referred, was a very natural characteristic of the motley shifting community of fishermen, seal hunters, sailors, smugglers and picaroons, who made the Isles of Shoals their rendezvous, and their home. Too remote from the mainland to be within effective reach of the feeble governments established there; able to set the law and its officers at open defiance, or to elude them by a ready escape into the open sea, these rude and hardy men would naturally despise all courts and their minions, and would come to look to their own sturdy right arms alone for the redress of grievances.[1]

We are aware that the Rev. Jedidiah Morse, author

[1] We may mention, in illustration of this spirit among the Islands, that some years ago, one of these stalwart Shoals fishermen was arraigned before the author, as a magistrate, upon a charge of "assault and battery." The man admitted frankly

of the brief "Description of the Isles of Shoals," printed in the 7th Vol. of the Mass. Hist. Coll., has described the population as, in early times, "industrious, prudent, temperate, and regular and decent in their attendance on the institutions of religion"; in which description he has been blindly followed by all the subsequent writers on the subject; but as we have now entered upon some account of the general character, habits, and social and religious condition of the islanders, it is proper to say, that we are compelled by the evidence on the subject, to dissent entirely from that writer's conclusions.

The class of virtues, which the learned divine ascribes to the Shoals community, in the times prior to the Revolution, not only seems inconsistent with the natural genius of such a community; utterly incongruous with the brave, but reckless and improvident character of "toilers upon the sea"; but also from the abundant evidence on the subject, which remains to us, it is precisely that class of virtues in which the islanders have ever been lamentably deficient.

that he had severely beaten the complainant in a square stand-up fight, but he set up, as a complete defence, that, in his own language, "they had agreed to heave the law one side." His rude sense of Shoals justice was sensibly shocked at a judgment against the sufficiency of his plea.

No one can, we think, decipher the ancient records of York county, of the township of Kittery, of Mass. Bay and New Hampshire, or peruse the writings and correspondence of the time, without perceiving that the pictures usually drawn of early society at the Shoals are very broad distortions of truth.

CHAPTER XIV.

ONE of the most remarkable peculiarities in the social condition of the Shoals, in very early times, was the exclusion by law of all women from inhabiting there. When and under what circumstances such a law was enacted, we are ignorant; but that an order of Court had been passed to that effect prior to 1647, we have the most controlling authority; while there is a probability, that the law was enacted even prior to the dissolution of the Company of Laconia in 1635. We know, from the records, that shortly after the dissolution, the law was treated as already obsolete, and women began to make their appearance in that community without objection. For instance, one of the grounds of complaint against Richard Gibson, the Shoals minister,[1] who was arraigned in Boston in

[1] Indeed, the parson himself, who resided at the Islands during 1641 and 1642, was a married man, and, we may presume, carried out his wife in his company. Mr. Gibson had, about 1637,

1642, was, in the language of Winthrop, that "he, being wholly addicted to the hierarchy and discipline of England, did exercise a ministerial function in the same way, and did marry and baptize at the Isle of Shoals, which was now found to be within our jurisdiction."[1]

Some excuse, if not justification, for the enactment of this singular rule of Court, may be found in the circumstances of the Shoals community in the earliest times. The original settlers, were, as we have remarked, young unmarried men; while the large number of transient fishermen, who entered the harbor during the summers, of course brought no women in their company. The strange females, therefore, who

while settled at Richmans Island, married Mary, daughter of Mr. Thomas Lewis, of Saco, and his life with her seems not to have been one of unruffled confidence and repose. In January, 1638, he writes to Gov. Winthrop, in a distracted state of mind, how that "some troublous spirits, out of misaffection, and others, as is supposed for hire, have cast an aspersion upon her, and generally avouch that she so behaved her self in the shipp, which brought her from England hither some two years agoe, that the block was reaved at the mayne yard to have duckt her, and that she was kept close in the ship's cabin 48 houres for shelter and rescue," and he therefore prays the Governor to take the testimony of several passengers in Boston, who came over in the same ship with his Mary, and "give a testimony of these Exacons." — 1 *Mass. Hist. Coll., 5th ser., p.* 267.

[1] 2 Winthrop, p. 66.

visited the islands in those days, must have been of a kind to provoke great disorder and licentiousness among the people, and in the end to justify their expulsion by law. But before long, the young men began to marry, and married men brought their wives over with them from Europe. The character of the community in this respect underwent a change, and the rule of Court against the fair sex gradually, by general consent, fell into oblivion.

In 1647, however, although there were at that time a considerable number of women residing at the Shoals, it was attempted to revive and enforce this now obsolete law. Richard Cutt and John Cutting, of the Isles of Shoals, petitioned the Court, held at "Pascataquack in the Province of Maine, in 1647, by his Excellency Henry Josselyn and the Associates," as follows:

"The humble petition of Richard Cutt and John Cutting, sheweth: that John Renolds, contrary to an Act in Court, that no woman shall live upon the Isle of Shoals, hath brought his wife thither, with an intention there to live and abide; and hath also brought upon Hog Island a great stock of goats and hogs, which doth not only spoile and destroy much fish, to the great damage of several others, and likewise many of your petitioners, but also doth spoile the spring of water, that is on that Island, by making it unfit or serviceable for any manner of use, which is the only relief and sustenance of all the rest of the Islands. Your petitioners, therefore, pray that the said Renolds may be ordered to remove his said goats and swine from the Islands forthwith. Also, that the Act of Court, before mentioned, may be put in execution, to the removal of all women from inhabiting there; and your petitioners shall pray, etc.

ORDER OF COURT ON THE ABOVE.

Whereas, by the above mentioned request, the general complaint of the chief of the fishermen and others, of the Isles of Shoals, that it is a great annoyance and prejudice for Mr. John Renolds to keep his swine and goats at the Isle of Shoals; it is by mutual consent of this Court ordered, that Mr. Renolds shall, within twenty days, remove his swine and goats that he hath at Hog Island from thence, or any of those islands that are inhabited with fishermen. And as for the removal of his wife, it is thought fit, if no further complaint come against her, she may as yet enjoy the company of her husband.

Dated the 20th day of October, 1647."[1]

Although, from the above petition and order, it appears that the fishermen of the Shoals were generally in favor of the expulsion of John Renolds' goats and swine, and although the petition was clearly drawn up by Cutts and Cutting, to be signed by "many petitioners," not a signature was procured by them for the expulsion of the women. Richard Cutt himself, although a large owner upon Star Island until his death, had at the time the petition was presented, already removed his residence to the Great House, at Strawberry Bank,[2] and thus was

[1] York County Court Records.

[2] 2 Mass. Records, p. 232.

restrained by no social terrors from this assault upon the women. Nor. is it likely that either he, or his brother John, were upon very friendly terms with the inhabitants of Hog Island or Smutty Nose. These two brothers were staunch adherents of Mass. Bay, and deeply tinctured with the Puritanical spirit; while the islanders, generally, were Royalists, Episcopalians, and at that time in open rebellion against the Massachusetts. It is thus probable, that the ungallant petition of Richard Cutt was a piece of spite against his former neighbors, in retaliation for the jibes and flings of the fishwives, who, as we shall hereafter see, were, like fishwives the world over, the mistresses of shrewd and biting tongues.

However this may have been, the married men of the Islands, when this obsolete law had been brought to notice, were not permitted to rest in peace, until it was expunged from the statute book. A petition for the repeal of the obnoxious law was presented to the Court by one William Wormwood, the hapless husband of Jane Wormwood, who had been already complained of as a common scold; and it was urged with such zeal, that at the General Court, held at Gorgeana, in 1650, "It was ordered, upon the petition of William Wormwood, that as the fishermen of the Isles of Shoals *will* entertaine womanhood, they have liberty to sit down there, provided they shall not sell neither wine, beare, nor liquor."[1]

We regret to add, that the "womanhood," thus licensed to sit down at the Shoals, did sometimes sorely abuse their privilege. Their offences generally consisted, it seems, in a singular volubility of tongue, and a certain asperity of temper.

For instance, at the Court held at Saco, in 1665, Joane Forde, wife of Stephen Forde, of the Isle of Shoals, was presented and convicted for "calling the constable Hornheaded rogue and Cowhead rogue."[1] "Joane Forde," continues the record, "was punished for this offence by nine stripes given her at the post, at a Court holden in York, Decem. 2, 1665."

Shortly afterwards, the same Joane Forde is presented, "for reviling and abusing the neighbors by very evil speeches; and for abusing the constable and other her neighbours." For this offence, Joane was "appointed to have ten lashes at the post, which was," says the record, "by John Parker, in presence of the Court, accordingly executed."[2]

In 1669, Mary Kelley, wife of Roger Kelley, of the Shoals, is presented "for abusing of her neighbours in an unseemly manner with badd words."

[1] York County Court Records.
[2] 1 Maine Hist. Coll., p. 375.

In 1666, Richard Down's wife is presented "for scoulding and abusing of her neighbours," and Gabriel Grubb's wife is brought before the Court "for slandering and abusing her husband."

Joane Andrews, the same year, is convented before authority, "for abusing of Mrs. Lockwood," and punished "with ten lashes on the bare skin at the whipping-post;" and Grace Tucker, the wife of William Tucker, of the islands, is convicted of abusing her neighbors "by evill and rayling speeches."

So serious and prevalent, indeed, was this sort of offence, that a law was enacted by the General Court, held at Gorgeana, in 1649, "that any woman, that shall abuse her husband, or neighborhood, or any other, by opprobrious language, being lawfully convicted, for her 1st offence, shall be put in the stocks two hours; for her 2nd offence, to be doucked: and if incorrigable, for to be whipped." [1]

For the proper infliction of the second kind of punishment, the Court ordered the erection in each town in Maine of a *cucking stool.* "This instrument," says Willis, "was reserved exclusively for scolds and brawling women; a class of offenders which modern times have permitted to go unpunished. It was a chair, suspended by a crane over water, into which

[1] York County Court Records.

the offender was plunged repeatedly, until her impatience and irritability were moderated. This species of punishment was quite popular, both in England and this country, in early days."[1]

The establishment of this infamous implement among the termigants of the Isles of Shoals was successfully resisted.[2] The cucking stool was not permitted to rise upon the breezy rocks of the Isles of Shoals, and the natural liberty of tongue, which the fishwives of Gosport and Hog Island seem to have prized so highly, was never afterwards assailed.

If the goodies and gammers of the Islands were sometimes guilty of intemperance of language, the men, on the other hand, were still more intemperate in the abuse of intoxicating liquors, the besetting sin of sailors and fishermen. The character given by old Josselyn to this class of people along the coast of Maine, is not, probably, overdrawn.

"These fishermen," writes he, about 1670, "often get in one voyage 8 or 9 pounds a man for their shares, but it doth some of them little good, for the merchant, to increase his gains by putting off his commodity, in the midst of their voyages, and at the end thereof, comes in with a walking Tavern, a Bark laden with

[1] 1 Willis Hist. of Portland, p. 117.

[2] Id.

the legitimate bloud of the rich grape, which they bring from Phial, Madera, Canaries, with Brandy, Rhum, the Barbadoes strong-water and Tobacco; coming ashore, he gives them a taster or two, which so charms them, that for no persuasions, that their employers can use, will they go out to sea, although fair and seasonable weather, for two or three days, nay, sometimes a whole week, till they are wearied with drinking, taking ashore two or three Hogsheads of Wine and Rhum, to drink off when the merchant is gone. If a man of quality chance to come, where they are roystering and gulling in wine with a dear felicity, he must be sociable and Roly-poly with them, taking off their liberal cups as freely, or else be gone, which is best for him; for when wine is at full tide, they quarrel, fight, and do one another mischief, which is the conclusion of their drunken compotations."[1]

The Puritan histories of Mass. Bay abound with the Special Providences visited upon the Shoals fishermen and their neighbors on account of this vice.

"April 20, 1658," writes Hubbard, "was observed to be the coldest night in all the year, in which two men, going from aboard a ship, which lay in Piscataqua River towards Kittery side, and being so drunk that

[1] Josselyn's Voyages to New England, p. 160.

they were not able to get to the ship again, were found next morning near the shore dead."

"June 5, 1666, one Tucker, a tailor, who belonged to the Isles of Shoals, being then at the point in Piscataqua River, was so drunk in the Lecture time, that, pulling off his clothes, he ran into the water, cursing and swearing, and was drowned." [1]

About that time, "two fishermen, after sermon on the Lord's day at Portsmouth, going into a house, drank so much rum, that being intoxicated therewith, they fell out of their canoe, as they were going down the river, and were both drowned."

"In June, 1671, one, J. S., having profanely spent the Lord's day, by passing to and fro from the Great Island to Kittery side, was so excessive drunk, that he fell over his canoe and was drowned, and his body not found till twelve days after."

"July, 1678, one Antipas Maverick, of the Isles of Shoals, being observed to be often overtaken with drink, at the last, in that distemper, fell out of his canoe and was drowned."[2]

"In Dec., 1633, one Cooper, of Pascataqua, going

[1] This was the same Tucker, we believe, whose house was so strangely washed away from Smutty Nose Island and carried to Cape Cod, in the great storm of 1635.

[2] Hubbard's Hist. of N. England, p. 597.

to an Island in the river there, to fetch sack to make merry on the Lord's day, was carried to sea and never heard of afterward. Thus they, that wander from the path of understanding shall, sooner or later, unless they return home by repentance, be found in the congregation of the dead."[1]

"In the year 1643, three fishermen, belonging to the Isles of Shoals, very profane and scorners of religion, being drinking all the Lord's day, the boat was cast away the next week and themselves all drowned."[2]

Others of similar "Remarkable Occurrents" may be found in Winthrop's History, Mather's Magnalia, etc.

The York County records also abound with evidence, as to the general abuse of intoxicating liquors among the Shoals people. We will only instance the case of Roger Kelly, of Smutty Nose, who in 1667, was presented at Court, for selling, without due license, to a party of ten fishermen, while "playing at ninepins on Hog Island," the quantity of "twelve gallons of wine, which they drank in one day."[3]

Large numbers of others among the fishermen were arraigned and convicted of being drunk, cursing, and swearing; and among that number are, naturally, enrolled the names of those hapless husbands, whose

[1] Hubbard's History of New England, p. 197.

[2] Id., p. 497.

[3] York County Records.

wives had been punished as "notorious and common scolds." Richard Downs, and Gabriel Grubb, and Tucker, and Andrews and Stephen Forde, among others, seem to have sought consolation in the bottle. They were all convented before authority, as being common drunkards, profane swearers and the like. John Andrews, the husband of scolding Joane, was convicted the same summer "for swearing, by the blood of Ch—t, that he was above the Heavens and the stars, at which tyme the said Andrews did seeme to have drunke too much and did at that time call the witnesses doggs, toads, and foul birds."

Without entering into further detail, we think our readers will be satisfied, from the illustrations already presented, that the inhabitants of the Isles of Shoals, in early times, were far indeed from being the "industrious, prudent, and temperate" people, they have been so often represented. Their virtues, like those of all communities similarily situated, lay in a widely different region of human character.

CHAPTER XV.

WHEN one of the New Hampshire ministers reproached his people, says Elliot, "that they had left the first purpose of their ancestors, who came to this howling wilderness to enjoy, without molestation, the exercise of pure principles of religion, one of his congregation interrupted him, saying truly: 'Sir, you entirely mistake the matter. Our ancestors did not come here on account of their religion, but to fish and trade.'"[1] The founders of the Isles of Shoals, such as we have described them, like those of Maine and New Hampshire in general, felt little sympathy with the religious tenets of New Plymouth and Massachusetts. Indeed, hardly more than one or two Congregational churches, after the New England model, had been gathered north of the Merrimac river, until after the country fell under the government of Massachusetts Bay.

[1] 1 Elliott's Hist. of N. England, p. 237.

Any attempt to introduce the Puritan form of worship among the Eastern people was considered hopeless. "There is noe possibility," writes William Hooke of Accominticus to John Winthrop in 1639–40, "of gathering a church here with us (after the Puritan fashion), except God in mercy open there eyes, and lett them see there supersticious waye, which they desier to goe.' "[1] The Eastern people, as to what religion they had, were thorough-paced Episcopalians, or conformists to the Established Church of England.

The Episcopal Church, at that period, contrasted itself from the sour austerities of the Reformers, by a genial patronage of gaiety and merriment, which commended it to the hearty favor of the sons of Mammon, who carried on fishing and trading around the Gulf of Maine. It encouraged maypoles, morris dances, wassails and junketings of all sorts; it smiled approvingly upon mince pies, cakes and ale, "bone lace and tiffany hoodes," and all manner of "bravery of apparel"; while, on the other hand, it discountenanced the intellectual vexations that tormented the fantastic dissenters of that day. Its consecrated service book supplied, ready always for use, a beautiful liturgy, which was amply sufficient

[1] 7 Mass. Hist. Col., 4th Ser., p. 197.

for all the spiritual needs of the rude population of the Eastern settlements.

The inhabitants of the Isles of Shoals adhered, accordingly, to the Established Church, until their annexation to Massachusetts Bay. Prior to 1640, the Rev. Joseph Hull, who was settled at Accominticus, visited the Islands occasionally and administered the sacraments in the chapel on Hog Island. During the year 1640, Rev. Robert Jordan, of Richmans Island, officiated in a similar way, and in 1641 and 1642, Richard Gibson, the first minister of Strawberry Bank, was settled at the Shoals. On Mr. Gibson's return to England in 1642, Joseph Hull, of Accominticus, renewed his occasional ministrations to the islanders, and as would appear from the inventory of his estate, maintained such relations until his death many years after.[1]

All these ministers were devoted adherents of the Established Church; and therefore, when the Shoals found it necessary or expedient to yield to the authority of the Massachusetts colony, one of the first measures, taken by the latter, was to send over to the Islands a sound Puritan divine. His name was John Brock, the first of a line of Congregational ministers,

[1] See the Inventory, in York County Rec., wherein a claim against the Islands for £20, for pastoral services, is set down among his assets.

who maintained that faith on the Shoals, until the decay of the settlement.

Rev. John Brock, though it seems probable that a portion of the inhabitants still adhered to their former pastor, Joseph Hull, was settled at the Shoals from about 1650 to 1662. "He dwelt as near Heaven," says Cotton Mather of him, "as any man upon earth. I scarce ever knew any man so familiar with the Great God, as his dear servant Brock."[1]

He was succeeded by the Rev. Mr. Hall, and the latter by Rev. Mr. Belcher. During the pastorate of the latter, the population of the northerly half of the Islands removed, as we have seen, to Star Island, on the New Hampshire side. The old church on Hog Island, which had now been standing upwards of half a century, was suffered to go to decay. In 1685 the northern half of the group was presented at Court "for their neglect in not maintaining a sufficient meeting house for the worship of God."[2] No heed seems to have been paid to this complaint; the chief part of the inhabitants having already removed, and erected a substantial new meeting house on Star Island, a building 28 by 48 feet, with a belfry and a bell. The loftiest point of the island was chosen

[1] 2 Mather's Magnalia, p. 32.

[2] York County Court Rec.

as the site of the building, in order that its elevated spire might serve as a landmark for mariners; in dark and tempestuous nights, the warning light may have gleamed from its belfry; and in times of fog, the groping fisherman was guided safely home by the note of its friendly bell.

Mr. Daniel Greenleafe was one of the first ministers of the new church. He was supported in part by contributions from the mainland, as will appear from the following vote of the New Hampshire Gen. Assembly in 1705: —

"The Representatives being informed that the General Assembly of the Massachusetts have given to Mr. Daniel Greenleafe, minister of the Isle of Shoals, fourteen pounds, provided this Province pay six pounds more for his support;"

"Voted that the Treasurer pay six pounds to Mr. Greenleafe for his encouragement in the ministry at Starr Island."[1]

When we consider that at this time there was a thriving community settled on Star Island, and that so considerable a contribution in those days as £20 was requisite for the encouragement of the Congregational ministry there, it seems clear that the population felt quite indifferent to religious concerns.

[1] 3 N. H. Prov. Pap., p. 319.

Mr. Greenleafe was succeeded, in 1706, by Mr. Moody, "a man of piety and a pathetic and useful preacher," who remained until 1733, when he was followed by Rev. John Tucke, the first minister regularly *ordained* to the congregation upon the Islands. He filled the pastoral as well as medical office until his death, in 1773, and in the words inscribed on his tombstone, at Star Island, "was a useful Physician both to the bodies and souls of his people."

During the pastorate of Mr. Tucke, the islanders certainly exhibited more of thrift and sobriety than they had ever shown before. His influence over them seems to have been strong and salutary. He was a man who attended to the material interests of his parishioners, as well as their spiritual welfare. He spent less effort in expounding abstruse dogmas they could not comprehend, than in inculcating morality and charity in the affairs of every day life.

His letter of acceptance of their call gave them fair warning that he should expect, or rather exact, a reasonable stipend for his services among them. "But, brethren," he writes, "I must say to you, as in 1 Cor., ix. 14: 'So hath the Lord ordained that they which preach the gospel should live of the gospel.' The same I expect amongst you." His parishioners seem to have appreciated highly this frank sort of dealing. They paid him the liberal salary of £100, Province money, besides promising further voluntary contributions; and for a part of his pastorate over them, from 1754 to 1771, they raised his salary to a quintal of "merchantable winter fish per man." As there were about one hundred men at that time on the Islands, and a quintal of fish was reckoned at a golden guinea, the salary was one of the highest at that time paid in New England.[1]

The Rev. John Tucke was buried on Star Island. His grave was accidentally discovered by Dudley A. Tyng, Esq., on his visit to the Shoals in 1800, and a monument erected to his memory, with a suitable inscription carved upon it.[2]

The Rev. Jeremiah Shaw succeeded Mr. Tucke in the ministry, and preached until the dispersion of the settlement, on the outbreak of the Revolutionary war. From that time to the close of the century, the ministrations of religion were suspended. So few were the numbers and so impoverished the circumstances of the islanders during that period, that "they had not the ability, and by degrees lost the disposition, to support the ministry. The people neglected the annual choice of town officers.

[1] 7 Mass. Hist. Coll., pp. 249, 256. Gosport Records.

[2] Tyng's manuscript Journal, p. 22.

They had no regular schools. The Sabbath was neglected and profaned. The vices of cursing and swearing, drunkenness, quarrelling and disobedience to parents became, in an awful degree, prevalent; and they were degenerating fast to a state of heathenism."

The marital relation was often entered into without the sacrament of marriage, and annulled at the whim of the parties, without the sanction of a divorce. A lamentable instance is to be found recorded at length by Rev. Jedidiah Morse in the town books, which sets this laxity in a clear, though painful light. Says the record: —

"Aug. 10, 1800. Thomas Mace was married to Hannah Randell, both of Gosport, alias Star Island, by

JEDIDIAH MORSE, V. D. M.

" Richard Randall was married to Nabby Robinson, both of Gosport, by JEDIDIAH MORSE, V. D. M.

" The two couple, above mentioned, had been published eight or ten years ago (but not married), and cohabited together since, and had each a number of children. Mr. Mace had been formerly married to another woman who had left him and cohabited with her uncle, by whom she has a number of children. No regular divorce had been obtained. Considering the peculiar, deranged state of the people on these

Islands, and the ignorance of the parties, it was thought expedient in order, as far as possible, to prevent future sin, to marry them."

So profound had their ignorance become, that some years afterwards, one of their missionaries, Mr. Caleb Chase, found it impossible to make a record of their ages, as all memory on that subject had been lost; according to tradition, their very language had so degenerated, as to be understood with difficulty by the people of the mainland.

The parsonage house, constructed for Mr. Tucke, was taken down by his son-in-law, and carried away to Old York in 1780; and as appears from the Gosport town records, the meeting-house itself, which had stood during nearly the whole 18th century on Star Island, having been erected at the expense of the islanders, about the year 1720, was wantonly set on fire, about 1790, by a gang of fishermen, who held a wild revel by its light until it consumed to ashes.[1]

The following entry of this circumstance on the Gosport Town Records was made by the Rev. Jedidiah Morse, during his visit to the Shoals in 1800: —

"About the year 1790, some of the people of the baser sort, not having the fear of God before their

[1] Gosport Town Records.

eyes, pulled down and burnt the meeting-house, which was a neat and convenient building, and had been greatly useful, not only as a place for religious worship, but as a landmark for seamen approaching this part of the coast. The special judgments of Heaven seem to have followed this piece of wickedness to those immediately concerned in it, who seem since to have been given up to work all manner of wickedness with greediness.

"By means of the exertions and benevolence of the Society for Propagating the Gospel, established in Boston, and some liberal minded gentlemen in Newburyport, Portsmouth and other places, there is a prospect and hope that another place of worship will be erected on the site of the old one, and the means of religious and moral instruction be again regularly afforded to the unfortunate and almost forsaken people of these Islands.

"Star Island, alias, Gosport,

"August 10, 1800."

The new meeting-house was built under the supervision of Dudley A. Tyng, Esq., the collector of the port of Newburyport; the necessary funds were obtained by the voluntary contributions of humane people along the coast. Five hundred dollars were subscribed in Salem, three hundred in Portsmouth, about one hundred in Exeter, and the remainder, about five hundred dollars, was taken up in Boston and Newburyport. The Rev. Dr. Morse interested himself deeply and efficiently in procuring these benevolences, and also in providing for the spiritual and temporal welfare of the Shoals people for many years after. The new meeting-house was somewhat smaller than the former one, being but 36 by 24 feet on the outside, two feet thick, and eleven feet high in the clear. The walls, which are still standing, were built of stone, a material which was preferred by Dr. Morse, as having, in his own words, "two great advantages over wood. The inhabitants *cannot burn it for fuel*, and it will be imperishable."

The new meeting-house was completed and dedicated by Rev. Jedidiah Morse, on the 24th Nov., 1800. The interior wood-work was partially destroyed by fire on Jan. 2, 1826, but shortly after was restored by the bounty of religiously disposed people on the mainland, and dedicated anew in 1830.[1] In 1859, the steeple of the church was adorned with a vane, to the high and mighty pride and satisfaction of the islanders. The

[1] The foregoing particulars concerning the meeting-house have been obtained from the manuscript Journal of Mr. Tyng, now in my possession.

glowing entry of this transaction on the town records is as follows: "At a considerable expense, the inhabitants of these Isles have put up a *beautiful vane* on our chapel. May their own hearts yield to the breathings of the Divine Spirit, as that vane does to the wind."

The meeting-house was, according to the original design, used during week days as a school-house, when a school has been maintained, and has always proved of great service as a landmark. When not required for the purposes of religion or instruction, it has been sometimes turned to good account by the islanders, it is said, in the drying and storing of codfish.

CHAPTER XVI.

SINCE 1800, the pulpit of the Shoals has been filled by missionaries, supported by religious associations on the mainland.

In 1799, the ancient "Society for Propagating the Gospell among the Indians and others in North America" sent out to the Islands, the Rev. Jacob Emerson, of Reading, as a pastor and schoolmaster; he remained there about three months. The next year (1800), the same Society procured Rev. Jedidiah Morse, the distinguished geographer, historian, and divine, to make an enquiry into the state of the people at the Shoals, and report as to the expediency of sending over another missionary and schoolmaster among them. Mr. Morse spent five days on the Islands, and preached four times, and distributed a number of books among them. On this occasion he also gathered up all the historical facts and traditions, not yet fallen into oblivion, and on his return to Charlestown, prepared for the Mass. Hist. Collections, that valuable article on the Isles of Shoals, to which subsequent enquirers have been so deeply indebted. By his recommendation, the "Society for Propagating the Gospel," etc., continued to send out missionaries for many years to the Islands.

It is not within the design of this sketch to set forth the long catalogue of worthy and pious men (some thirty in number), who now succeeded each other, at brief intervals, in the pastoral office, until the extinction of the settlement. We may only venture to extract from the numerous reports of these missionaries to the mother Society such particulars concerning the social and domestic condition of the islanders during the last half century, as may interest the general reader.[1]

Mr. Josiah Stevens, one of the first of the missionaries, married, in 1802, Susanna, daughter of Mr. Samuel Haley, Jr., of Smutty Nose, and in consequence of this connection and his interest in the people, he was willing to be engaged as a permanent minister,

[1] In the year 1841, the Rev. T. B. Fox, at that time settled in Newburyport, compiled, mostly from these Reports, a very interesting and accurate account of the then condition of the Islands. This account, together with all the other historical matter gathered by him, including the manuscript Journal of Dudley A. Tyng, Mr. Fox has most kindly contributed to our use in these pages.

From the "Society for Propagating the Gospel," and from individuals, he received a salary of $300 per annum. By the exertions of Mr. Tyng, money enough was raised, and articles given by the charitable, in the town and elsewhere, to build and furnish a parsonage house on the very spot where the house of Mr. Tucke had stood. Mr. Stevens received a commission from the State of New Hampshire, as a Justice of the Peace; and appears to have acted with vigor in his office. In one of his letters to Mr. Tyng, he asks for a pair of "stocks," and from a subsequent communication to the same gentleman, we learn that he received and used, with good effect, those now antiquated instruments of punishment for evil doers. But he was removed in the midst of his usefulness by death, July 3d, 1804, aged 64.

One of the later missionaries was Mr. Reuben Moody, a theological student, who remained a few months in the spring of 1822. "We have been favored," continues Mr. Fox, "with extracts from a journal kept by Mr. Moody. They are, most of them, of a character too private for publication. But to show what was the state of society at that time, we venture to give a few items. Under date of April 1st, he says, — 'Mr. —— came into my room and asked when I intended to open my school? I answered, I could not before I had wood; and that I was not authorized to purchase any; but if the people were willing to purchase it, and find me a room, I was ready to commence it any day. After about three hours he sent a message to me, to come and view a room. I found he had provided wood and seats in a small but convenient room. He said, this is all I can do; here is the key, and you may open your school as soon as you please. He afterwards gave me his reason for it: '*that his children made such a disturbance at home, he could not sleep in the day time.*' Again: April 20 — 'My school presents a singular appearance in the morning. As soon as they see me with my brand of fire and key, they all leave their plays and run; and when I am building the fire they flock round me and squat down on the hearth like *pappooses.* Some with their books, some with their Indian bread, and some with none.' "

In another part of the journal there is an account of an old man, who lived alone and drank forty gallons of rum in twelve months. But there is even a worse story than this to be told. "I am informed," says Mr. Moody, June 17th, "that one poor person's rum bill, for one month past, amounts to four gallons he has carried home, and 175 gills drank at the house of a person for whom he fishes. The person with whom I board informs me that since I have been here, he has drawn out two barrels of rum; and he has but two hired men, his wife, and a child thirteen months old, who with himself compose his family. Since the first of April, his brother has drawn out seven barrels of rum. Admitting the other persons, four in number, who sell rum, to have retailed as much, in less than three months more than six hundred gallons of rum have been drank here. The Island contains 65 inhabitants; of these 24 are under the age of twelve, 10 are females, who have not all drank a gallon since I have been here: subtracting these, there remain 31; to these add 16 hired men—making 47 men, whose average allowance has been 12 gallons and 3 quarts to a person, or about 5 gills per day."

"Mr. Origin Smith, one of the late missionaries," continues Mr. Fox, writing in 1841, "first visited the Shoals Aug. 26, 1835. Since June, 1837, he has been permanently settled at the Shoals with his wife and family. Mr. Smith is supported in part by the Society for Propagating the Gospel—in part by the Rev. Mr. Peabody's parish, in Portsmouth, N. H. — in part by the Islanders — and in part by donations from individuals in this town. A few extracts from Mr. Smith's Reports, and a letter to the Rev. Dr. Parkman of

Boston, will give the reader an idea of the present condition of the Shoals, and of the improvement that has taken place among them. In 1840, Mr. Smith says — " The people of my charge seem to be willing to do what they can for my support, yet they are able to do but little. For the past year they have raised forty dollars for my salary, and about ten dollars to procure fuel for the School and Sabbath. * * *

" The cause of temperance is slowly advancing. About forty belong to the Temperance Society, which excludes all intoxicating liquors. The person who sold spirits the past year, has abandoned the sale, joined our Society, delivered an excellent address to the people, and pledged his future influence on the side of temperance. There is one man here who keeps spirit to sell to strangers and water parties; but he does not sell to the inhabitants on the Islands. There are four or five drunkards on all the Islands, and four who call themselves 'moderate drinkers.' There are five men and five women who never attend public worship — three of the men, however, will frequently come and sit on the steps of the meeting-house and listen to what is said; but we cannot prevail upon them to enter the sanctuary."

In 1855, Rev. J. Mason was the missionary upon the Islands, and in his report to the Society for Propagating the Gospel, etc., gives an interesting account of the character and condition of his people at that time.

"The kind of business which the people pursue," writes Mr. Mason, "affects unfavorably their habits, physical, social, and religious. Family discipline is neglected; religious duties in the household performed (if attended to at all), irregularly and in haste; and much time, apparently wasted, is spent in watching for favorable indications to pursue their calling.

"But the people express their approval and appreciation of what is doing for them in a way peculiar to themselves — one evening, unsolicited, 'taking up a collection' of five dollars, made up of very 'small change,' to pay Mr. Mason 'for lighting the house'; another evening a similar sum 'for more fuel for the singing school'; and again surprising us unceremoniously by putting a barrel of extra fine flour, a leg of bacon and a bucket of sugar into our back kitchen, saying, 'our neighbors have sent you this.' Such expressions of regard towards their minister should not be overlooked; for 'their deep poverty abounded unto the riches of their liberality.'

"We hope that our example, as well as instructions, while mingling with the people by their own firesides and in our domestic arrangement, has not been lost. I never refused to render aid, when solicited, even in making a coffin for the dead; and Mrs. Mason has had the privilege of exercising her taste, and trying her skill upon 'coats and garments,' probably not very dissimilar to those 'which Dorcas made.'

"In the relations they sustain to the missionary, they require of him more than is just and proper. He must have the whole care of the public buildings. This includes repairing, cleansing and preserving from injury. On the Sabbath and in the day schools, I have made, during two years past, all the fires, swept the buildings, rang the bell or hoisted the 'Bethel flag.' Furthermore, unconscious of any impropriety, they have sought the missionary to mow their grass, file their saws, repair their clocks, pull their teeth and make coffins for the dead. I speak of these insignificant matters only to give you an insight into some peculiarities of this people.

"In conclusion, I would add that to withdraw those humane Christlike influences, which your Society have, through so long a period, exerted on this population, however slight the impressions felt, would be ruinous. Their degeneracy into a kind of civilized heathenism would be rapid, and the Shoals would soon show one of the most desolate, hopeless moral wastes in New England."[1]

[1] Report of Soc. for Prop. the Gospel among the Indians, etc., for year 1855.

Several other missionaries succeeded to Mr. Mason, one of the last of whom was Rev. George Beebe, whose wife discharged for a time the duties of school-mistress. The Rev. Mr. Barber succeeded Mr. Beebe in 1867, and was followed in 1869 by the last of the long line of missionaries, the Rev. Mr. Hughes. For two years past, the pulpit has had no incumbent, and one by one the little band of parishioners has passed away from the Islands.

CHAPTER XVII.

THE aversion of the Islanders, as well as of Maine and New Hampshire generally, towards the Puritan form of worship, was, in the early times, to which we now return, no doubt deepened by their hostility to the political principles of the Massachusetts. The founders of these Eastern parts were staunch royalists throughout the whole course of the English Rebellion. Many, if not most of them, had emigrated from Bristol, Dartmouth, and other parts of the southwest of England, which long held out for Prince Rupert, and fell at last struggling stoutly for the Royal cause. Both Mason and Gorges, the patentees of New Hampshire and Maine, were active royalists, and the latter laid down his life in the King's service.

The civil and religious dissensions between the two wings of New England, during the Great Rebellion, ran almost as high as in the mother country itself. The commission of the Earl of Warwick, Lord High

Admiral for the Long Parliament, was openly acknowledged in Boston, and his ships of war allowed to make prize of the King's vessels in the harbor; while, on the other hand, the warrant of Prince Rupert, Admiral for the King, was recognized at the Eastward as the only lawful authority; and the "harp and cross" ensign of the Parliament was regarded as little better than piratical.

It is obvious, that between the loyal, Episcopalian sons of Belial, who inhabited the Isles of Shoals, during the times especially of the first planters, and the Puritan Commonwealth men, who "set up their Ebenezer" at Massachusetts Bay, intense antipathy must have existed. It would be curious, if not amusing, to quote a few additional passages from the Puritan writers of the time in illustration of that spirit.

Says Thomas Jenner, in 1640, the people of the Eastern settlements "are generally very ignorant, superstitious, and vicious, and scarce any religious."[1]

Thomas Dudley, of Boston, relates that some of his fellow-immigrants, in 1630, proving "desperately wicked, hearing of men of their own disposition, which were planted at Piscataway, went from us to them; whereby, though our numbers were lessened,

[1] 7 Mass. Hist. Coll., 4th Ser., p. 355.

yet we accounted ourselves nothing weakened by their removal."[1]

Hubbard, the minister of Ipswich, tells us, how the stout old soldier, Captain Underhill, of Dover, being questioned, in 1638, before the Court at Boston, for saying "that they at Boston were zealous, as the Scribes and Pharisees were, and as Paul was before his conversion," was laid under an admonition, "and how," continues the historian, "like a prophane person, as was sometimes said of Cain, he went from the presence of the Lord, and dwelt on the East of Eden, so this gentleman went to the Eastward, and made a great bluster among the inhabitants of Exeter and Dover."[2]

Many similar expressions of antipathy and contempt may be found in Winthrop and other early Bay writers. The Rev. Mr. Hubbard, indeed, seems to have considered our Eastern affairs as entirely beneath his notice.

"How great a sound soever," he writes, "is or hath been made about the Province of Maine, and the land about Piscataqua river, the whole history thereof may be compressed in a few words, so far as anything may

[1] Young's Chronicles, p. 315.

[2] Hubbard's New England, p. 353.

be found in either of them, worthy to be communicated to posterity."[1]

Daniel Neal, another of the Puritan historians of New England, writing some forty years later than Hubbard, seems to have entertained a similar contempt for our Eastern settlements. His entire account of the Provinces of Maine and New Hampshire, although professing to write a History of New England, is compressed into two sentences, both of which are conspicuous for inaccuracy. He dismisses us as follows: —

"The next Province (to Nova Scotia) is New Hampshire, which is bounded by Kennebec river on the east, and Merrimack river on the west. In the midst of this Province is the County of Main, which, as I observed before, belongs to the Massachusetts, and contains the following considerable towns: Falmouth, Hedeck or New Castle, Edgartown, York, the Isles of Shoals, etc." [2]

On the other hand, the invectives of the Eastern people against the Massachusetts, though not, perhaps, as decorous in language, were not at all inferior in meaning and unction.

[1] Hubbard's New Eng., p. 213.

[2] 2 Neal's Hist. of New England (Ed. 1720), p. 578.

A Piscataqua man, being in England, in 1632, said of the Massachusetts planters, "they would be a peculiar people to God, but all goe to the Devil; they are a people not worthy to live on God's earth; fellows that keep hoggs all the week, preach there on the Sabbath; they count all men, out of their church, as in the state of damnation, etc."[1]

John Josselyn, of Black Point, writes of the founders of Boston, "the chiefest objects of discipline, Religion and morality, they want; some are of a Linsie-woolsie disposition, of several professions in religion; all, like the Aethiopians, white in the teeth only, full of ludification and injurious dealing, and cruelty, the extremest of all vices. Great Syndies or censors or controllers of other men's manners, and savagely factious among themselves."[2]

So, too, hard-drinking Thomas Warnerton, of Strawberry Bank, in 1644, declared in his wrath, "they were all rogues and knaves at the Bay, and he hoped to see all their throats cut; and they had no law for the Eastern people but to starve them."[3]

In brief, in the scriptural expressions of the time, the Eastern people abhorred Massachusetts, "as Hadad

[1] 6 Mass. Hist. Coll., 4th Ser., p. 486.

[2] Josselyn's Voyages to N. England, p. 188.

[3] 1 Mass. Rec., p. 152.

the Edomite abhorred Israel," while, in return, the Puritans felt "a call and a rule" to smite the Phillistines at the east, "hip and thigh," upon all suitable occasions. There was an irreconcileable repugnance between them; in temper, disposition, habit, as well as in political and religious principles—a lack of sympathy which endures, to some extent, even to the present day.

The character of the New England Puritan, or even of the Separatist of New Plymouth, is painfully sterile to the fancy, and dreary to the feelings. The crushing severity of their social and sumptuary laws, the sanctimonious formality of their daily intercourse, the jading monotony of their religious bigotry, blighted nearly every flower and sweet-scented herb, with which Providence has cheered and adorned human life.

The spirit of our islanders, as well as of the early founders of New Hampshire and Maine in general, was in broad contrast, at all points, with that of the Puritans. Their virtues lay in the rugged domain of daring, fortitude, frank honesty and generosity of heart—robust English virtues, which, on Captain Smith's "heape of rocks," enjoyed a free development into lawless and extravagant forms, it may sometimes be, but at the same time into a richness and a raciness, highly pleasing to the taste.

CHAPTER XVIII.

THE golden age of the Isles of Shoals, to which we now recur, was the middle of the seventeenth century. Their population was at that time larger than at any other point in the Eastern provinces; trade and commerce were extensive; the fisheries were pursued with activity; the little harbor was filled with shallops and pinnaces; the neighboring sea was dotted with sails, sweeping in and out; the rocks, now so silent and deserted, resounded with clamor and bustled with business, — everywhere boisterous hilarity, animal enjoyment, exuberant spirits, cheerful and varied activity.

It was a motley population, with all the reckless and improvident habits of sailors and fishermen, and with all their hardihood, courage and spirit of adventure — a dauntless race, accustomed to contend against the most tremendous and appalling forces of Nature, when to quail or to tremble was to be lost. Their "fearful trade" taught them such lifelong lessons of self-reliance, as almost to obliterate from their minds the very sense of Divine protection and aid.

"During the ministry of Rev. Mr. Moody," relates Mr. Morse, "one of the fishing shallops, with all hands on board, was lost in a N. E. storm in Ipswich Bay. Mr. Moody, anxious to improve this melancholy event, for the awakening of those of his hearers, who were exposed to the like disaster, addressed them in the following language, adapted to their occupation and understanding:

"'Supposing, my brethren, any of you should be caught in the bay, in a N. E. storm, your hearts trembling with fear, and nothing but death before you, whither would your thoughts turn? What would you do?'

"'What would I do?' replied one of these hardy sons of Neptune,' 'why, I should h'ist the fores'l and scud away for Squam.'"

"While Mr. Brock resided at the Shoals," runs another anecdote, "the fishermen came to him, on a day devoted to the worship of God, and requested that they might put by their meeting that day, and go a-fishing, because they had lost many days by the foulness of the weather. He pointed out to them the impropriety of their request, and endeavored to convince them that it would be far better for them to stay at home and worship God, than to go a-fishing. Notwithstanding his remonstrance, however, five only consented to stay at home, and thirty determined to go. Upon this, Mr. Brock addressed them thus: 'As for you, who are determined to neglect your duty to God, and go a-fishing, I say unto you, Catch fish, if you can. But as for you, who will tarry and worship the Lord Jesus Christ, I will pray unto him for you, that you may catch fish till you are weary.' Accordingly the thirty who went from the meeting, with all their skill, caught through the day but four fishes; while the five, who tarried and attended divine service, afterwards went out and caught five hundred."[1]

Whatever faith we may put in this Special Providence, we may safely believe the thirty profane fishermen to have been guilty of the offence charged. It is not the way of fishermen, the world over, to listen attentively and reverently to the parson's homily, while the fish are schooling around them. We are told by Sir Walter Scott, that in one of the Hebrides islands, it is quite canonical to break up the church service at once, on the appearance of a whale blowing in the offing.[2]

[1] 7 Mass. Hist. Coll., p. 251.

[2] It is, however, a point of honor that none of the parishioners should leave the church porch, until the curate has had time to strip off his surplice and come down to the door, so that all might have a fair start.

The deeper mysteries of religion were utterly incomprehensible to our ignorant fishermen; the subtle distinctions, between sanctification and justification, between the covenant of works and the covenant of faith, which employed the pulpits of the Puritans, were to the people of the Shoals the dreariest jargon; while the restraints of the forms and observances of worship were altogether intolerable to their impatient natures.

Neither was the shifting, heterogeneous character of the population conducive to sobriety or stability. These barren rocks were the resort of the Letter of Marque, and the pirate, who in early days infested the Gulf of Maine; of the whaler and seal hunter, and of many a refugee and runagate from the old world. Cavaliers, on the downfall of the Royal cause, may have here found convenient hiding; and perhaps some ship of Prince Rupert's fleet, scattered and broken in West India waters, may have here, among sympathizing friends, found refuge and means to refit.

It must needs have been a picturesque spot in those early times. In the sunny summer days, when the wind failed, great hulking fishermen, in red Monmouth caps, leathern jerkins and clumsy boots, lolling listlessly about the rocks, smoking Brazil tobacco, and waiting patiently for a breeze — fishwives garrulously mending nets in the sun — ragged urchins at their boisterous games up and down the lanes of the hamlet — groups of idlers hanging around the ordinaries and ale houses — long flakes spread with drying fish — the harbor dotted with ketches and pinnaces at anchor — the smoking cottage chimneys — the glittering sea — the distant coast line dozing in a blue haze.

By-and-by the blue catspaws are seen on the ocean, the breeze freshens, and within a half hour the whole scene changes. Away to the east and north the vessels scatter and disappear. Hardly an able bodied man is left on the Islands. The settlements are left in guard of women. Silence settles down on the rocks, broken only by shrill voices, or the occasional yelp of some village cur. The Islands await in silence the fishermens' return.

As the twilight comes on, the fishing boats, one by one, come winging home. The wind has hauled out to the eastward, a fog rolls in behind them, the weather looks threatening. And now many a Bylander, caught creeping along the neighboring coast, shallops, pinnaces, ketches and fleets of fishing craft of every kind, scud into the harbor for a night's refuge; and it is not long before the silent rocks resound with revelry.

Taverns and ale houses abounded on all the Islands, and we may be sure their walls echoed with the hoarse hilarity of the outlandish company, as they quaffed their tankards of beer, their passado or Barbadoes strong waters, or "took off their liberal cups of rhum-bullion;" while, as they drank and smoked Brazil tobacco, some weather-beaten salt would spin the marvellous yarn, or recount

> " Such wonderful stories of battle and wrack,
> As are told by the men of the watch."

Or else, one of the chanters of the fishermen would pipe up, in a high key, some old forecastle ditty, or some ancient fishing song, that he learned in England:

> "Oh, the herring he loves the merry moonlight,
> The mackerel loves the wind,
> But the grampus he loves the fisherman's song,
> For he comes of a gentle kind."

Meantime Scozway, the Micmac Indian, who was the best fiddler along the coast,[1] would tune up his strings, and on the bare tavern floor the young men and women would dance the Brantle, the fore-and-aft reel, or the famous country dance of England, called "Cuckolds all awry." And thus, as the jargon grew louder, while the bowl went about, the hours would pass away until the fog lifted or the storm was spent.

But now nothing except the tumbled walls of a ruined and abandoned hamlet, so rare to see in New England, remain to attest the former existence upon

[1] Josselyn's Voyages, p. 106.

these celebrated Islets, of the busy and boisterous settlement we have pictured. With the decline of the fisheries, the population have departed, and the sea-mews, after an absence of two centuries, have returned to their ancient haunts.

"A heape of rocks" was the first English description of the Isles of Shoals — "a heap of crags," strangely enough, is also the last. In the fine language of Lowell:—

> "A heap of bare and splintery crags,
>   Tumbled about by lightning and frost,
> With rifts, and chasms, and storm-bleached jags,
>   That wait and growl for a ship to be lost.
> No islands ; but rather the skeleton
> Of a wrecked and vengeance-smitten one."

APPENDIX.

We have thought proper to print as an Appendix to the foregoing pages, the following copies of documents on file at the office of the Secretary of State, New Hampshire, as they shed important light upon certain periods of the Shoals' history. These documents will be fouud, we think, to support the views embodied in the text, and may be of particular interest to the antiquary.

To his Excellency Sam'l Shute, Esq., Captain Generall, Governm'r and Commander in Chief in and over his Magesties Province of New Hamp., &c.

To the Honourable the Councill and Representatives Conven'd in Gen'll Assembly, now settling in Portsm'o in sd Province.

The Petition of Richard Yeaton, one of the Selectmen of Starr Island upon the Isles of Shoales in behalfe of the Inhabitants thereof most humbly sheweth —

That the Selectmen of the sd Island have not expressed any contempt to the Authority by their omitting to make an assessment on the people thereof pursuant to the Treasurers Warrant, aud therefore humbly prays that your Excellency and the Honourable Assembly would pass a favorable construction thereon, and also prays that your Excellency and this Honourable Assembly would be pleased to consider the following pleas in favour of their being excused from the Province Tax.

The people are very few in number and most of them are men of no substance, live only by their daily fishing, and near one third of them are single men and threaten to remove and leave us, if the tax be laid, which will prove our utter ruin if our ffishermen leave us.

The charge and expence which they are at in the support of the ministry is as great as the people can bear at present, it having cost them but lately the sum of Two Hundred pounds for that end in building a Meeting House — which is not yet all paid.

The Government have heretofore encouraged them that they should be exempted from paying Province Taxes, whilst they exprest their forwardness in so good a service.

Though the Inhabitants have been very much richer and more numerous and their Trade greater than at present, yet they were not then rated, nor the Inhabitants on the Islands in the Massachusetts Government.

They live on a Rock in the Sea, and have not any Privilege of right in Common Lands as other Inhabitants in the respective Towns have.

They have defended themselves in the time of Warr ag'st the publick enemy at their own expence both for forts and souldiers whose wages they have paid; and finally all other Towns in their Province have been larger and more numerous before they were taxed to the Province rate.

I do with a humble confidence assure your Excellency and the Honourable Assembly that we shall ever express a loyalty to his Majesty and a ready obedience to the commands of the Government, but considering our poverty with the foregoing pleas in our favour, I do humbly pray that you will please to excuse us from the present Tax, and when we shall be better capable shall readily bear our proportion of the publick charge — and so your Petitioner shall ever pray, as in duty bound, &c., and subscribe

RICH'D YEATON.

22*d April* 1721.

PROVINCE OF NEW HAMPSHIRE } *To his Excellency Benning Wentworth, Esq. Captain General, Governour and Commander in Chief in and over the said Province, the Hon'ble His Majestys Council and House of Representatives in General Assembly conven'd, January 4th*, 1760.

Humbly Shew — Henry Carter, Richard Talfrey and Charles Miller all of Gosport within said Province in behalf of themselves and the other inhabitants of said Gosport, that the said Inhabitants have allways chearfully paid their Province Tax with great willingness and pleasure so long as they were of ability and until the fonr last years when their circumstances in life became so low (being a few poor fishermen) and the necessaries for living being excessively dearer at the place of their abode one half more than at any other part of the Province with the great difficulty of Transporting the same there, together with their other great charge supporting the Gospel ministry among them, the fewness of the Inhabitants and their poverty, and their few within four years last past being Greatly Reduced, they having had Thirty-Two Ratable poles within that time left them to serve the King or Removed to other places, Six of which had familys, and there is but few very few young men among them and the neighboring Islands in the Mass. Bay altho very short of our number have on account of their poverty been exempted from Tax for Twenty years last, and altho Warrants from the Treasurer have come to the selectmen of said Gosport to assess the Inhabitants for their part year after year yet the selectmen did only the first year assess them and on finding that was not paid the poverty of the Inhabitants and some Great Encouragement from Some of the Honble General Court that on shewing forth the Difficulties aforesaid the same might be Remited and since they have not made any assesment for Province Tax, and that that was made was never colected and now the same amounts to a very considerable Sum, and if their very few and remaining Inhabitants should be oblidged to pay the same it would greatly tend to their Ruin, for the few remaining young men would Remove from them Rather than pay any part of such back taxes as were due before some of them were oblidged by law to pay any, and their would be none but a few old helpless persons left, and we would here beg leave to observe to this Honble Court that had we had a representative in Court at the time the proportion was made, Gosport might not have been Taxe'd. But altho we were always informed that we were allow'd the Liberty of sending one member to Represent us in said Court yet we never asked it, knowing it would be a great cost to the Province more than any advantage of Tax that could possibly be expected from the Inhabitants, for which Reason we never made any Enquiry into the matter.

Wherefore We Humbly pray the consideration of this Honble Court on the premises, and that you will be pleas'd to pass such an Act or Resolve to take of the said Back Tax's and that we may be exempt for the time to come, or grant such other Relief therein as in your Great Wisdom shall seem meet unto you, and then we from such Incouragement shall have Great Reason to hope that instead of our few becoming fewer we shall increase in our numbers and be able to pay Province Taxes with great willingness when we shall have it in our ability — and, by being heard in this our Request we shall as in Duty Bound ever pray

HENRY CARTER
RICHARD TALFREY } *Selectmen.*
CHARLES MILLER

In Council, Jan'ry 4th, 1760, read and order'd to be sent down to the Hon'ble Assembly.

THEODORE ATKINSON, *Sec'y.*

PROVINCE OF NEW HAMPSHIRE } *In the house of Representatives June 5th* 1761. *This Petition being read*

Voted, That the prayer thereof be granted, and that the sum of five hundred and Twelve pounds Eight shillings and one penny new Tenor, that appearing to be the sum due from Gosport for the province Tax be Remitted, and that the Treasurer he hereby Intitled to charge the said sum to the Province.

A. CLARKSON, *Clerk.*

£512 8 1 new Tenor.

In Council June the 16 — 1761.

Read and Concurred.

THEODORE ATKINSON, *Sec'y.*

Consented to

B. WENTWORTH.

To his Excellency Benning Wentworth Esq'r. Lieut General, Governor and Commander in Chief in and over his Majesty's Province of New Hampshire, the Hon'ble his Majesty's Council and House of Representatives for said Province in General Assembly Convened the 25th day of June, Anno Domini 1766.

The Humble Petition of the Inhabitants of Gosport in the Province of New Hampshire and others whose Interest is concerned — shews —

That the situation of the Road and harbour at Gosport aforesaid is well known to be exposed to the violence of Winds and Seas in many cases and Events which frequently occur by which they often sustain much Loss and Damage which they wou'd gladly Prevent if by any means feasible.

That it has been Judg'd a Pier or Bason might be so contrived and built as to be in a Great measure a security in this case and a means of great saving to your Petitioners and Preservation of their Property.

That to make such a work effectual a Larger sum would be demanded than your Petitioners by any means cou'd raise, but as it wou'd be of very General Utility in its consequence, they flatter themselves the scheme for carrying on such a Building wou'd meet with suitable Encouragement from many other Persons besides your Petitioners and those who have connections with them.

Wherefore your Petitioners Humbly Pray that they may have leave to set up and carry on a Public Lottery to raise money for the End aforesaid and for that Purpose to bring in a bill containing such Limitations and Restrictions as shall be tho't necessary but with such extent and authority as shall be sufficient to Effect the Design and your Petitioners as in Duty bound shall ever Pray, &c.

Jno. Tucke.
Henry Carter.
Richard Talfrey.
John Varrell(?)
William Mickamore.
William Holbrook.
Henry Shapley.
Richard Talfrey, Jun'r.
Henry Talfrey.
Daniel Rindle.
James Hickey.
Samuel Varrell.

Samuel Varrell, Jun'r.
John Down.
John Down, Jun'r.
Samuel Downe.
Jeremiah Lord.
Jos. Damrell.
Peter Robinson.
John Walfrey.
Ambrose Perkins.
John Barter.
Wm. Sanderson.
George Walfrey.
Josiah Sanderson.
Henry Shapley, Jun'r.
Joseph Muchamore.
Elamuel Muchamore.
Benj'n Muchamore.
Sam'l Muchamore.
Arthur Rendle.
Arthur Rendle, Jun'r.
George Rendle.
John Rendle.
Edward Bondey.
Henry W. Andrews.
S. Mathews.
Jno. Newton.
Stephen Pierce.
Jas. Ward.
Rich'd Langford.
Wm. Bickam(?)
Sam'l Healy.
John Parrell.
Sam'l Currier.
Sam'l Muchmore.
Gregory Purcell(?)
Sam'l Cutts.
Daniel Rindge.
Geo. Boyd.
Nath'l Adams.
Jonathan Warner.
Thomas Wentworth.
John Sherburne.
D. Sherburne.
Sam'l Warner.
Titus Salter.
Abraham Trefethen.
Hugh Hall Wentworth.
Wm. Knight.
Temple Knight.
Samuel Sherburne.
Geo. Janvrin.
Sam'l Dalling.
John Flagg.
Joseph Whipple.
James Stoodly.
Rich'd Hart.
Wm. Whipple.
Jno. Parker.
H. Wentworth.
John Penhallow.
Thos. Bell.
Samuel Moffatt.
D. Peirce.
Paul March(?)
John Moffatt.

PROVINCE OF NEW HAMPSHIRE } *In Council June* 28, 1766, *Read and Ordered to be sent down to the Hon'ble Assembly.*

T. ATKINSON, JUN., *Sec'y.*

PROVINCE OF NEW HAMPSHIRE } *In the House of Representatives, July 3d,* 1766.

Voted, That the Petitioners be heard on this Petition the second Day of the siting of the General Assembly after the first of September next, and that the Petitioners at their own cost cause the substance of this Petition and Order of Court to be Published three weeks successively in the New Hampshire Gazett that any Person may appeal and shew cause why the Prayer thereof should not be granted.

M. WEARE, *Clr.*

In Council Eod'm Die
read and Concurred
T. ATKINSON JUN., *Sec'y.*

PROVINCE OF NEW HAMPSHIRE } *In the House of Representatives Aug'st 28th* 1767.

The foregoing Petition being Read and Considered, appearing Reasonable and no objection made,

Voted, That the Prayer of the Petition be Granted and that the Petitioners have Liberty to bring in a Bill accordingly.

M. WEARE, *Clr.*

In Council Eod'm Die
Read and Concurr'd
T. ATKINSON, JUN., *Sec'y.*

In the House of Representatives, Sept. 17, 1767, P. M.

An act for granting a Lottery for building a Pier or Bason at the Isle of Shoals having been three times Read

Voted, That it pass to be Enacted.

Sent on by Mr. Bailey.

Sept. 24, 1767.

Mr. Sec'y bro't from the Board the Act for granting a Lottery for building a Pier or bason at the Isles of Shoals, and said the Councill tho't the managers appointed by the Act ought to be under Oath, which by the Act they were not obliged to; and Proposed that amendment to be made.

The House considering the amendment proposed agreed that it be made, which being made, the Act was sent to the Board again.

Journal of Council and Assembly, Sept. 24, 1767.

A Bill Intituted An Act for granting liberty to carry on a Lottery to raise money for building a Pier and forming a Bason in the Harbour at Gosport. Read a 3d time and past to be Enacted, and assented to by the Governor.

THEODORE ATKINSON, JUN., *Sec'y.*

This scheme of raising funds, by lottery, for the construction of a pier or basin at the Shoales, having proved impracticable, was shortly after abandoned.

www.ingramcontent.com/pod-product-compliance
Lightning Source LLC
LaVergne TN
LVHW011227110826
845150LV00006B/1567